THE VOICE FROM ON HIGH

GOD ANNOUNCES HIS SON AS ISRAEL'S LIBERATING KING
FROM GENESIS TO REVELATION

RETOLD BY

CHRIS SEAY, BRIAN MCLAREN, LEONARD SWEET, LAUREN WINNER
and others

the voice™

A SCRIPTURE PROJECT TO REDISCOVER THE STORY OF THE BIBLE

THOMAS NELSON
Since 1798

NASHVILLE   DALLAS   MEXICO CITY   RIO DE JANEIRO   BEIJING

www.thomasnelson.com

The Voice from on High
Copyright ©2007 Thomas Nelson, Inc.

Published in Nashville, Tennessee, by Thomas Nelson. Thomas
Nelson is a trademark of Thomas Nelson, Inc.

Published in association with Eames Literary Services,
Nashville, Tennessee

Typesetting by Rainbow Graphics
Interior photography by Kelly Jackson Photography
(www.kellyjackson.com)

Printed in the United States of America

07 08 09 10 11 12 13 14 15—9 8 7 6 5 4 3 2 1

Contributors
The Voice from on High

Scriptures retold by:

David Capes	Kelly Hall	Chris Seay
Don Chaffer	Chad Karger	Allison Smythe
Lori Chaffer	Phuc Luu	Leonard Sweet
Greg Garrett	Brian McLaren	Kristin Swenson
Amanda Haley	Jonathan Hal Reynolds	Lauren Winner

Reflections by: Jonathan Hal Reynolds

Scholarly review by:

Darrell Bock	Dave Garber
David Capes	Sheri Klouda
Alan Culpepper	Creig Marlowe
Peter Davids	Chuck Pitts
J. Andrew Dearman	Felisi Sorgwe
Brett Dutton	Nancy de Claissé Walford

Editorial review by:

Amanda Haley
Maleah Bell
Kelly Hall
Merrie Noland
James F. Couch, Jr.
Marilyn Duncan

A SCRIPTURE PROJECT TO REDISCOVER THE STORY OF THE BIBLE

Table of Contents

Preface

Any literary project reflects the age in which it is written. **The Voice** is created for and by a church in great transition. Throughout the body of Christ, extensive discussions are ongoing about a variety of issues including style of worship, how we separate culture from our theology, and what is essential truth. In fact, we are struggling with what is truth. At the center of this discussion is the role of Scripture. This discussion is heating up with strong words being exchanged. Instead of furthering the division over culture and theology, it is time to bring the body of Christ together again around the Bible. Thomas Nelson and Ecclesia Bible Society together are developing Scripture products that foster spiritual growth and theological exploration out of a heart for worship and mission. We have dedicated ourselves to hearing and proclaiming God's voice through this project.

Previously most Bibles and biblical reference works were produced by professional scholars writing in academic settings. **The Voice** uniquely represents collaboration among scholars, pastors, writers, musicians, poets, and other artists. The goal is to create the finest Bible products to help believers experience the joy and wonder of God's revelation. Four key words describe the vision of this project:

- holistic   considers heart, soul, and mind
- beautiful   achieves literary and artistic excellence
- sensitive   respects cultural shifts and the need for accuracy
- balanced   includes theologically diverse writers and scholars

Uniqueness of *The Voice*

About 40 different human authors are believed to have been inspired by God to write the Scriptures. **The Voice** retains the perspective of the human writers. Most English translations attempt to even out the styles of the different authors in sentence structure and vocabulary. Instead, **The Voice** distinguishes the uniqueness of each author. The heart of the project is retelling the story of the Bible in a form as fluid as modern literary works yet remains true to the original manuscripts. First, accomplished writers create an English rendering; then, respected Bible scholars adjust the rendering to align the manuscript with the original texts. Attention is paid to the use of idioms, artistic elements, confusion of pronouns, repetition of conjunctives, modern sentence structure, and the public reading of the passage. In the process, the writer or scholar may adjust the arrangement of words or expand the phrasing to create an English equivalent.

To help the reader understand how the new rendering of a passage compares to the original manuscripts, several indicators are embedded within the text. Italic type indicates words not directly tied to a dynamic translation of the original language. Material delineated by a ruled box expands on the theme. This portion is not taken directly from the original language. To avoid the endless repetition of simple conjunctives, dialog is formatted as a screenplay. The speaker is indicated, the dialog is indented, and quotation marks are not used. This helps greatly in the public reading of Scripture. Sometimes the original text includes interruptions in the dialog to indicate attitude of the speaker or who is being spoken to. This is shown either as a stage direction immediately following the speaker's name or as part of the narrative section that immediately precedes the speaker's name. The screenplay format clearly shows who is speaking.

Throughout **The Voice,** other language devices improve readability. We follow the standard conventions used in most translations regarding textual evidence. **The Voice** is based on the earliest and best manuscripts from the original languages (Greek, Hebrew, and Aramaic). When significant variations influence a reading, we follow the publishing standard by bracketing the passage and placing a note at the bottom of the page while maintaining the traditional chapter and verse divisions. The footnotes reference quoted material and help the reader understand the translation for a particular word. Words that are borrowed from another language or words that are not common outside of the theological community (such as baptism, repentance, and salvation) are translated into more common terminology. For clarity, some pronouns are replaced with their antecedents. Word order and parts of speech are sometimes altered to help the reader understand the original passage.

—Ecclesia Bible Society

About *The Voice* Project

As retold, edited, and illustrated by a gifted team
of writers, scholars, poets, and storytellers

A New Way to Process Ideas

Chris Seay's (president of Ecclesia Bible Society) vision for **The Voice** goes back 15 years to his early attempts to teach the Bible in the narrative as the story of God. As Western culture has moved into what is now referred to as postmodernism, Chris observed that the way a new generation processes ideas and information raises obstacles to traditional methods of teaching biblical content. His desire has grown to present the Bible in ways that overcome these obstacles to people coming to faith. Instead of proposi- tional-based thought patterns, people today are more likely to interact with events and individuals through complex observations involving emotions, cognitive processes, tactile experiences, and spiritual awareness. Much as in the parables of Jesus and in the metaphors of the prophets, narrative communication touches the whole person.

Hence, out of that early vision comes the need in a postmodern culture to present Scripture in a narrative form. The result is a retelling of the Scriptures: **The Voice,** not of words, but of meaning and experience.

The Timeless Narrative

The Voice is a fresh expression of the timeless narrative known as the Bible. Stories that were told to emerging generations of God's goodness by their grandparents and tribal leaders were recorded and assembled to form the Christian Scriptures. Too often, the passion, grit, humor, and beauty has been lost in the translation process. **The Voice** seeks to recapture what was lost.

From these early explorations by Chris and others has come **The Voice:** a Scripture project to rediscover the story of the Bible. Thomas Nelson and

Ecclesia Bible Society have joined together to stimulate unique creative experiences and to develop Scripture products and resources to foster spiritual growth and theological exploration out of a heart for the mission of the church and worship of God.

Traditional Translations

Putting the Bible into the language of modern readers has too often been a painstaking process of correlating the biblical languages to the English vernacular. The Bible is filled with passages intended to inspire, captivate, and depict beauty. The old school of translation most often fails at attempts to communicate beauty, poetry, and story. *The Voice* is a collage of compelling narratives, poetry, song, truth, and wisdom. *The Voice* will call you to enter into the whole story of God with your heart, soul, and mind.

A New Retelling

One way to describe this approach is to say that it is a "soul translation," not just a "mind translation." But "translation" is not the right word. It is really the retelling of the story. The "retelling" involves translation and paraphrase, but mostly entering into the story of the Scriptures and recreating the event for our culture and time. It doesn't ignore the role of scholars, but it also values the role of writers, poets, songwriters, and artists. Instead, a team of scholars partner with a writer to blend the mood and voice of the original author with an accurate rendering of words of the text in English.

The Voice is unique in that it represents collaboration among scholars, writers, musicians, and other artists. Its goal is to create the finest Bible products to help believers experience the joy and wonder of God's revelation. In this time of great transition within the church, we are seeking to give gifted individuals opportunities to craft a variety of products and experiences: a translation of the Scriptures, worship music, worship film festivals, biblical art, worship conferences, gatherings of creative thinkers, a Web site for individuals and churches to share biblical resources, and books derived from exploration during the Bible translation work.

The heart of each product within **The Voice** project is the retelling of the Bible story. To accomplish the objectives of the project and to facilitate the various products envisioned within the project, the Bible text is being translated. We trust that this retelling will be a helpful contribution to a fresh engagement with Scripture. The Bible is the greatest story ever told, but it often doesn't read like it. **The Voice** brings the biblical narratives to life and reads more like a great novel than the traditional versions of the Bible that are seldom opened in contemporary culture.

Readable and Enjoyable

A careful process is being followed to assure that the spiritual, emotional, and artistic goals of the project are met. First, the retelling of the Bible has been designed to be readable and enjoyable by emphasizing the narrative nature of Scripture. Beyond simply providing a set of accurately translated individual words, phrases, and sentences, our teams were charged to render the biblical texts with sensitivity to the flow of the unfolding story. We asked them to see themselves not only as guardians of the sacred text, but also as storytellers, because we believe that the Bible has always been intended to be heard as the sacred story of the people of God. We assigned each literary unit (for example, the writings of John or Paul) to a team that included a skilled writer and biblical and theological scholars, seeking to achieve a mixture of scholarly expertise and literary skill.

Personal and Diverse

Second, as a consequence of this team approach, **The Voice** is both personal and diverse. God used about 40 human instruments to communicate His message, and each one has a unique voice or literary style. Standard translations tend to flatten these individual styles so that each book reads more or less like the others—with a kind of impersonal textbook-style prose. Some translations and paraphrases have paid more attention to literary style—but again, the literary style of one writer, no matter how gifted, can unintentionally obscure the diversity of the original voices. To address these problems, we asked our teams to try to feel and convey the diverse literary styles of the original authors.

Faithful

Third, we have taken care that **The Voice** is faithful and that it avoids prejudice. Anyone who has worked with translation and paraphrase knows that there is no such thing as a completely unbiased or objective translation. So, while we do not pretend to be purely objective, we asked our teams to seek to be as faithful as possible to the biblical message as they understood it together. In addition, as we partnered biblical scholars and theologians with our writers, we intentionally built teams that did not share any single theological tradition. Their diversity has helped each of them not to be trapped within his or her own individual preconceptions, resulting in a faithful and fresh rendering of the Bible.

Stimulating and Creative

Fourth, we have worked hard to make **The Voice** both stimulating and creative. As we engaged the biblical text, we realized again and again that certain terms have conventional associations for modern readers that would not have been present for the original readers—and that the original readers would have been struck by certain things that remain invisible or opaque to modern readers. Even more, we realized that modern readers from different religious or cultural traditions would hear the same words differently. For example, when Roman Catholic or Eastern Orthodox readers encounter the word "baptism," a very different set of meanings and associations come to mind than those that would arise in the minds of Baptist or Pentecostal readers. And a secular person encountering the text would have still different associations. The situation is made even more complex when we realize that *none* of these associations may resemble the ones that would have come to mind when John invited Jewish peasants and Pharisees into the water of the Jordan River in the months before Jesus began His public ministry. It is far harder than most people realize to help today's readers recapture the original impact of a single word like "baptism." In light of this challenge, we decided, whenever possible, to select words that would stimulate fresh thinking rather than reinforce unexamined assumptions. We want the next generation of Bible readers—whatever their background—to have the best opportunity possible to hear God's message the way the first generation of Bible readers heard it.

Transformative

Finally, we desire that this translation will be useful and transformative. It is all too common in many of our Protestant churches to have only a few verses of biblical text read in a service, and then that selection too often becomes a jumping-off point for a sermon that is at best peripherally related to, much less rooted in, the Bible itself. The goal of **The Voice** is to promote the public reading of longer sections of Scripture—followed by thoughtful engagement with the biblical narrative in its richness and fullness and dramatic flow. We believe the Bible itself, in all its diversity and energy and dynamism, is the message; it is not merely the jumping-off point.

The various creations of the project bring creative application of commentary and interpretive tools. These are clearly indicated and separated from the Bible text that is drawn directly from traditional sources. Along with the creative resources and fresh expressions of God's Word, the reader has the benefit of centuries of biblical research applied dynamically to our rapidly changing culture.

The products underway in **The Voice** include dynamic and interactive presentations of the critical passages in the life of God's people and the early church, recorded musical presentations of Scripture originally used in worship or uniquely structured for worship, artwork commissioned from young artists, dramatized audio presentations from the Gospels and the Old Testament historical books, film commentary on our society using the words of Scripture, and exploration of the voice of each human author of the Bible.

The first product for **The Voice**, entitled *The Last Eyewitness: The Final Week*, released Spring 2006, follows Jesus through His final week of life on earth through the firsthand account of John the apostle. This book combines the drama of the text with the artwork of Rob Pepper into a captivating retelling of Jesus' final days. The second product, *The Dust Off Their Feet: Lessons from the First Church*, was released September 2006 and includes the entire Book of Acts retold by Brian McLaren with commentary and articles written by nine scholars and pastors. *The Voice of Matthew* was released January 2007 with the Gospel of Matthew retold by Lauren Winner including Lauren's devotional commentary, along with cultural and historical notes. *The Voice of Luke: Not Even Sandals,* released June 2007, contains the Gospel of Luke retold by Brian McLaren and includes his devotional notes.

The Voice Revealed: The True Story of the Last Eyewitness, a fall 2007 release, is the full Gospel of John retold by Chris Seay in a compact edition to introduce others to the faith. *The Voice of Hebrews: The Mystery of Melchizedek* includes a retelling of the Book of Hebrews by Greg Garrett with extensive notes and articles by David Capes. *The Voice of Mark* retold by Greg Garrett with commentary by Matthew Paul Turner will complete the products for the winter.

The Team

The team writing **The Voice** brings unprecedented gifts to this unique project. An award-winning fiction writer, an acclaimed poet, a pastor renowned for using art and narrative in his preaching and teaching, Greek and Hebrew authorities, and biblical scholars are all coming together to capture the beauty and diversity of God's Word.

Writers

The writers for **The Voice** are:

Eric Bryant—pastor/author
David Capes—professor/author

Don Chaffer—singer/songwriter/poet
Lori Chaffer—singer/songwriter/poet
Tara Leigh Cobble—singer/songwriter
Robert Creech—pastor/author
Greg Garrett—professor/author
Christena Graves—singer
Sara Groves—singer/songwriter
Amanda Haley—archaeology scholar/editor
Charlie Hall—singer/songwriter
Kelly Hall—editor/poet
Greg Holder—pastor
Justin Hyde—pastor/author
Andrew Jones—pastor/consultant
E. Chad Karger—counselor/author/pastor
Tim Keel—pastor
Greg LaFollette—musician/songwriter
Evan Lauer—pastor/author
Phuc Luu—chaplain/adjunct instructor
Christian McCabe—pastor/artist
Brian McLaren—pastor/author
Donald Miller—author
Sean Palmer—pastor
Jonathan Hal Reynolds—poet
Chris Seay—pastor/author
Robbie Seay—singer/songwriter
Kerry Shook—pastor
Chuck Smith, Jr.—pastor/author
Allison Smythe—poet
Leonard Sweet—author
Kristin Swenson—professor/author
Phyllis Tickle—author
Matthew Paul Turner—author/speaker

Lauren Winner—lecturer/author
Seth Woods—singer/songwriter
Dieter Zander—pastor/author

Scholars

Biblical and theological scholars for *The Voice* include:

Joseph Blair, ThD—professor
Darrell L. Bock, PhD—professor
David B. Capes, PhD—author/professor, HBU
Alan Culpepper, PhD—dean/professor
Peter H. Davids, PhD—pastor/professor
J. Andrew Dearman, PhD—professor
J. R. Dodson, MDiv—adjunct professor
Brett Dutton, PhD—pastor/adjunct professor
Dave Garber, PhD—professor
Mark Gignilliat, PhD—assistant professor
Charlie Harvey, PhD—assistant professor
Peter Rhea Jones, Sr., PhD—pastor/professor
Sheri Klouda, PhD—professor
Tremper Longman, PhD—professor
Creig Marlowe, PhD—dean/professor
Troy Miller, PhD—professor
Frank Patrick, MDiv—assistant professor
Chuck Pitts, PhD—professor
Brian Russell, PhD—associate professor
Felisi Sorgwe, PhD—pastor/professor
Nancy de Claissé Walford, PhD—professor
Kenneth Waters, Sr., PhD—professor
Jack Wisdom, JD—lawyer

Introduction

Introduction

I am not a huge fan of choral music, but it is not from lack of exposure—
I have been to more than my share of choral events, concerts, and festivals. I entered Baylor University on a vocal performance scholarship, sang
as a featured baritone in the Baylor Chorus, and attended the required 40
hours of recitals per semester. But on more than one occasion, I was denied
credit for recital attendance due to the alleged offense of blatantly sleeping
through the event. In the last 16 years, I have not come within sight of any
choral event, with a single exception—George Frideric Handel's *Messiah*.

I first experienced Handel's *Messiah* at the age of nine, the same year I
heard the Christian band Whiteheart and witnessed their newfangled laser
light show. If the two experiences are compared, the honest truth is that the
1980s glam rock band was forgettable while the auditorium filled with old
people, sheet music, and choir robes left an impression on me that changed
the course of my spiritual journey. Handel's work compelled me a quarter-
century ago, and to this day it stands alone as one of the most profound
spiritual experiences of my lifetime. Please don't tell my uber-cool friends
in the emerging church, but if I had to choose between a Switchfoot concert
and a *Messiah* sing-along, I'd choose the *Messiah* sing-along every single
time without hesitation.

Messiah takes me on a spiritual and emotional journey that begins in
isolation and leads me through fiery trials, despair, hopelessness, fear, and
torment; and it inexplicably points me toward the embodiment of all truth
in Jesus the Liberating King, note after note. There has never been a more
complete artistic expression of the gospel than the *Messiah* by George Frideric Handel.

Handel, if living today, would be the premier postmodern evangelist—
the postmodern Billy Graham, if you will. Why is that? Because he tells the

whole story of the gospel through art, beauty, and story. He manages to leave no stone unturned. It is all there: creation, pain, hope, redemption, sin, longing, healing, and celebration. The only theme that repeats itself time and again is the incarnation of the Liberating King.

The great King Solomon despairs that we will not learn from men of old. I am hoping he is wrong in this instance because we have so much to learn from our brother, George Frideric Handel. Through a collaborative effort, Ecclesia Bible Society and Thomas Nelson bring you this exploration of the Scriptures inspired by the verses Handel used in his artistic and evangelistic masterpiece known as *Messiah.*

We've included a sampler CD with selections from *Songs from The Voice, Volumes 1 and 2,* featuring Lori Chaffer, Jill Paquette, Tyler Burkum, and others. To truly experience this book, I suggest listening to the songs indicated beneath the section titles as you read. By immersing ourselves in these Scriptures and our most recent musical interpretations of them, I believe we will discover a meaningful path for the church in a new age.

So sit back, put on your headphones, and embark on a journey of hope, love, and renewal told through the beautifully interwoven music and Scripture that just might show us how to be the body of Christ in a postmodern world.

Hallelujah, and Glory to God in the Highest!

Chris Seay

Section One

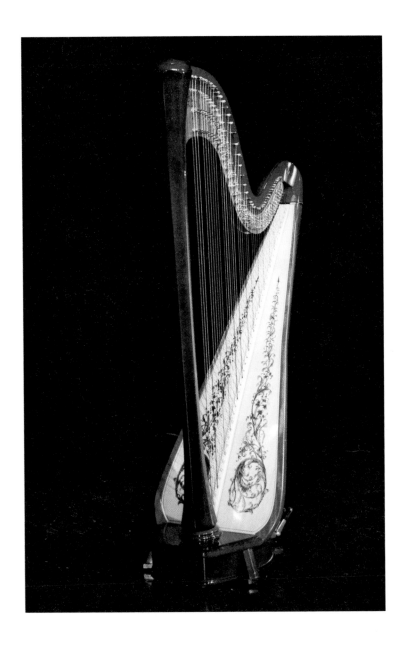

The Eternal Song
(He Will Not Rest)

An eternal song is playing. Before the first flash of light interrupted the darkness, it was there. Before the first tug of gravity pulled the heavenly bodies into a celestial dance, it filled the cosmos. Before raging waters carved deep valleys through rock mountains, it thundered like a waterfall. The Bible bears witness to this song that tells the story of one True God—the Creator, Composer, and Conductor of the great oratorio of redemption. In each movement we hear the music that changes the world forever. This clear, singular melody describes God's love and His great mercy. Biblical writers performed it with the instruments of ancient poetry, parables, letters, and reports of visions contained in our Scripture. It is a melody of love, wonder, war, and redemption. Its meaning (if one's heart and ears are open to it) transcends all time and space and raptures the human soul with its divine sound.

From Genesis to Revelation we hear this melody that God composed for His creation. To appreciate the message behind these many different texts and the themes that hold them together, we must hear this underlying melody performed by the many different human authors inspired by the voice of God.

Imagine the story of Scripture as a grand oratorio performed on the stage of the universe. God is the Composer of the work in all its parts. The Holy Spirit is the Conductor of this breathtaking work, and the Liberating King is the enchanting Vocalist of the piece; all movements, all action from before the first flicker of light began to spiral outward to reach this tiny rock called earth, lead to His performance in the final act.

It is the beginning; the stage is set. God places humanity in a lush paradise called Eden, where the first man and woman enjoy a life of unbroken communion with their Creator. For a time, they walk through wild gardens, play in crystal rivers, sleep beneath an audience of stars; they are never far from His watchful eye. But they abandon God's melody to follow the counter-rhythm, sin, sacrificing paradise by disobeying God and eating the forbidden fruit. The map to Eden is lost. The key to its gate is destroyed. The first family and all their descendants are separated from perfect intimacy with God, our Maker. Creation shudders and waits.

Many generations after humanity has forgotten Eden and God's perfect song, a man named Abraham arrives on the stage; and God, the Eternal One, chooses him to be His ambassador to the fallen world. God takes Abraham outside one night and says, "Look up at the stars, and try to count them all if you can. *They are too many to count!* But your descendants will be as many as the stars."[1] In the deep of night Abraham enters into a covenant with the Eternal One: God promises Abraham innumerable descendants and the land of Canaan as long as his sons and daughters demonstrate their devotion to God by faithful obedience.[2] The Lord pledges that Abraham's family will be a blessing to all the families of the world. The renewal of creation is underway. God extends this covenant with Abraham's descendants, including Moses and King David to whom a special promise is made: the Liberating King will be David's Son. Scores of prophets foresee His arrival.

Generation after generation, the children of Israel expect the glorious arrival of their Liberating King. Based on the declarations of their prophets, they await a ruler who will establish justice and bring universal peace. But they read more, and less, into the prophe-

[1] Genesis 15:5; 22:17
[2] Genesis 17:1-16

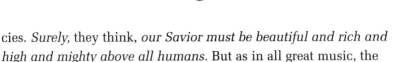

cies. *Surely,* they think, *our Savior must be beautiful and rich and high and mighty above all humans.* But as in all great music, the composition moves in a direction the listeners don't fully expect.

A simple carpenter of mysterious, divine heritage enters the scene. In Him all the dissonance of the ages is resolved. In Him all the hopes of displaced people rest. He is God's Messiah, our Liberating King. He speaks in riddles and creates a new world with parables. He repairs the old world with miracles and heralds the coming of God's great and glorious kingdom. The people shout and sing, "Hosanna, blessed is the one who comes in the name of the Lord!"[3]

But some people still dance and move to their old comfortable rhythms. They look upon our Liberator in disbelief and disgust because this humble, poor man spends time with common fishermen and washes the dirt from their feet. To the displeasure of power brokers everywhere, He invites the entire human race to enter God's coming kingdom, a scandalous and paradoxical way of being. Who is this man? He incites revolution, transformation, and devotion, not by force but by fierce spiritual awakening. He offers the hope of a new reality to the entire world—that earth might become like heaven, a hopeless chaos transformed into a kingdom of hope.

As the melody plays, the leaders among men reject this simple preacher. They accuse Him of blaspheming God's name, violating God's law, and being in league with God's enemies. They attempt to silence Him by hanging Him upon a cross and leaving Him to die—nails piercing His wrists and feet. Little do they know that their love for power and hate for Him are part of God's plan. Because they've misunderstood what was to come, these leaders cannot understand that this man, Jesus, is the sacrifice required for the redemption of their own imprisoned souls. Despite all the charges

[3] Matthew 21:9; Mark 11:9; John 12:13

against Him, despite the tragedy of His death, His followers come to believe the unbelievable. Three days later when He reappears alive and well, they understand His true identity as their Liberating King.

As time elapses, the words of Jesus are proven true. His coming divides humanity. Millions of people follow the Liberator's ways and work toward establishing His kingdom on earth. But others abandon His wisdom, reject His liberation, and are bound in the comfort of sin. As Jesus predicted, the kingdom suffers violence at the hand of those intent on following the counter-rhythm of sin. But there's more to the prophecies than they imagine. Once again, the Liberating King must enter the stage and complete His mission.

We know from the prophets and Jesus' followers that our Liberating King will return a second time, fully defeating sin, judging humanity, and establishing His perfect kingdom—the kingdom God intended. In this final act, God will restore the world to its original glory and grandeur. The last will be as the first, when He heals every disease, wipes away every tear, and subdues all His enemies. The delight of Eden will return, and dry places will become springs of living water. As for humanity, the crown of His creation, He will take our deep flaws—our utter brokenness—and redeem us. Created by Him and for Him, we will commune with Him, free from the threatening counter-rhythm of sin.

*T*he music begins before the first atom of the cosmos is formed. It springs from the heart of the One God who is always creating, always composing. It is a melody of beauty and truth. But in that time before time, God is not alone. Before the first flash of light chases away the darkness, there is community in the One God. The Voice is with Him, and through Him all creation dawns. This is the One who would someday liberate us all. So He steps into our world, becoming like us to reveal God's glory and truth.

John 1:1-5, 14-18

[1]Before time itself was measured, the Voice was speaking. The Voice was and is God. [2]This *celestial* Voice remained ever present with the Creator; [3]His speech shaped the entire cosmos. *Immersed in the practice of creating,* all things that exist were birthed in Him. [4]His breath filled all things with a living, breathing light. [5]Light that thrives in the depths of darkness, *blazing through murky bottoms*. It cannot, and will not, be quenched.

[14]The Voice *that had been an enigma in the heavens chose to* become human and live surrounded by His creations. We have seen Him. Undeniable splendor enveloped Him—the one true Son of God— *evidenced in* the perfect balance of grace and truth. [15]John, *the wanderer* who testified of the Voice, introduced Him. "This is the one I've been telling you is coming. He is much greater than I because He existed *long* before me." [16]Through this man we all receive *gifts of* grace beyond our imagination. *He is the Voice of God.* [17]You see, Moses gave us rules to live by, but Jesus the Liberating King offered the gifts of grace and truth *which make life worth living*. [18]God, unseen until now, is revealed in the Voice, God's only Son, *straight from* the Father's heart.

Millennia separate creation from the Voice's entrance into our story. When God first creates the cosmos, everything is in perfect harmony. The world is a beautiful garden; and we spend our days working the good earth, tending the trees, and communing with God. Life is a simple melody.

Genesis 2:4-9

[4]This is the *detailed* story of the Eternal God's *singular work in* creating all that exists. On the day the heavens and earth were created, [5]there were no plants or vegetation to cover the earth. The fields were barren and empty with no life or growth because the Eternal God had not sent the rains *to nourish* the soil or a man to tend the soil. [6]In those days a fog rose from the soil and its vapors irrigated the land. [7]One day He scooped dirt out of the ground, sculpted it into the shape *we call* human, and breathed into the nostrils *of the body to fill the human creation with life. When the human body met the divine breath,* a soul was born.

[8]The Eternal God planted a garden in the east *and called it* Eden— *for it was a place of utter delight*—and placed the man there. [9]*In this garden* He made the ground pregnant with life—*bursting forth with nourishing food and luxuriant beauty*. He created trees that ravished the eyes and yielded unimaginable delicacies. Among them stood the tree of life. And in the center of this garden *of delights* stood the tree of the knowledge of good and evil. *(But more about that later in the story.)*

God's creation is so amazing that it inspires us to create. Made in His image, fashioned in His likeness, we write songs celebrating its beauty and glorifying the majesty of its Creator. From His vantage, far above the earth, He is able to foresee humanity's path—that we will war among ourselves and abandon His perfect ways—so He plans the path of liberation even as He creates our world. He gives the humanity authority to rule creation, both when we are in the garden and when we are banished from it. He then sends us laws that will both bring us closer to Him and to each other, but sin ultimately exploits the laws to enslave us. He crowns some of us as kings just as one day He will crown the Liberator over all of us. That Liberator will be the perfect human, the Son of Man, our brother, who comes to restore the world and rule the creation God originally composed.

Psalm 8:1-9

[1]O Eternal One, our Lord,
>   Your majestic name is heard throughout the earth,
>   *inscribed into the very fabric of creation;*
>   Your magnificent glory shines far above the skies.

[2]From the mouths *and souls* of infants and toddlers,
>   *the most innocent,*
>   You have decreed power to stop Your adversaries
>   and quash those who seek revenge.

[3]When I gaze to the skies and meditate on Your creation—
>   on the moon, stars, *and all* You have made,

⁴I can't help but wonder why You care about mortals—
    sons and daughters of men—
    specks of dust floating about the cosmos.

⁵But You placed the son of man just beneath God
    and *honored him like royalty*
    with a crown of glory and majesty.

⁶You ordained him to govern the works of Your hands,
    to nurture the offspring of Your divine imagination;
    You placed everything on earth beneath his feet:
⁷All kinds of domesticated animals,
    even the wild animals in the fields *and forests.*
⁸The birds of the sky and the fish of the sea,
    all the multitudes of living things that travel the currents of the
        oceans.

⁹O Eternal One, our Lord,
Your majestic name is heard throughout the earth,
    inscribed into the very fabric of creation.

---

*T*he perfect melody of creation does not last long. Our ancestors stray from God's composition and follow the counter-rhythm of a serpent's song instead of their Conductor's direction. It is this act of defiance that God foresees when He lays the path for the Liberator. But our sins lay a path as well—a path that leads to murder, war, and crimes against creation. These sins are so grievous, so heavy, that only God can lift them and eliminate them from the perfect creation.

From the beginning, the creation story is intertwined with the story of the Liberating King. A great drama begins in the garden with the most basic of conflicts between good and evil. Although God's creation was good, indeed very good, evil is present in the serpent who plays on the yet unrealized pride and curiosity of the man and the woman. Lies. Deception. The counter-rhythm of sin will drive humanity until the Liberating King arrives to restore humanity to the perfection God intended.

Genesis 3:1-24

[1]Of all the wild creatures the Eternal God had created, the serpent was the craftiest.

Serpent		*Dear woman,* is it true that God has forbidden you to eat fruits from the trees of the garden?
Woman	2	*No, serpent. He said* we may eat *freely. We are granted access to any variety and all amounts* of fruit in the garden [3]with one exception—the fruit from the tree found in the center of the garden. God instructed us not to eat or touch the fruit of this tree, so we would not experience certain death.
Serpent	4	*Die?* No, you would not die. *God is playing games with you.* [5]*The truth is,* God knows eating the fruit from that tree will awaken something powerful in you and make

you like Him: possessing *all* knowledge of things both good and evil.

[6]The woman *approached the tree,* eyed its fruit, and coveted its *mouthwatering, wisdom-granting* beauty. She plucked a fruit from the tree and ate. She then offered the fruit to her husband, and he ate as well. [7]Suddenly their eyes were opened *to a reality previously unknown*. For the first time, they *sensed their vulnerability and rushed* to hide their naked bodies, stitching fig leaves into a crude loincloth. [8]Just then, they heard the Eternal God walking in the cool shadows of the garden. They took cover among the trees.

Eternal God	9	*(calling to the man)* Where are you?
Man	10	I was hiding from You. I was afraid when I heard You coming.
Eternal God		*Why are you afraid?*
Man		Because I am naked.
Eternal God	11	Who told you that you are naked? Have you eaten from the tree *in the center of the garden*, the one I commanded you not to eat from?
Man	12	*(pointing at the woman) It was she!* The woman You gave to me put the fruit in my hands, and I ate it.

Eternal God	13	*(to the woman)* What have you done?

Woman It was the serpent! He tricked me, and I ate.

Eternal God **14** *(to the serpent)* What you have done carries great consequences. Now you are cursed more than cattle or other beasts. You will writhe on your belly forever, consuming the dust *out of which man was made.* [15]I will make you and your brood enemies of the woman and all her children; the woman's child will stomp your head, and you will bite his heel.

16 *(to the woman) As a consequence of your actions,* I am increasing your suffering—the pain of labor at childbirth and the sorrow of bringing forth the next generation. You will desire a husband; *but rather than a companion and collaborator,* he will be the dominant partner.

17 *(to the man)* Because you followed your wife's advice *instead of My command* to refrain from the fruit I had forbidden you to eat, cursed is the ground. For the rest of your life, you will fight for every crumb of food from the *crusty clump of* clay *I made you from.* [18]*Instead of sweet fruit,* the ground will now produce aggravating thorns and thistles, and you will eat the plants of the field. [19]Your brow will sweat for your mouth to taste even a morsel of bread until the day you return to the very ground I made you from. From dust you have come, and to dust you will return.

[20]The man named his wife Eve, because she was *destined to become* the mother of all the living. [21]The Eternal God wove together the skins of animals as clothes for Adam and Eve to wear.

| Eternal | 22 | Look, the human has become like Us, possessing the knowledge of good and evil. *If We don't take action,* he might take fruit from the tree of life, eat it, and live forever . . . |
| God | | |

Before finishing that thought, the Eternal God acted. [23]He sent the couple out from the garden of Eden *and exiled humanity from paradise, sentencing humans* to a laborious life working the very ground from which they came. [24]Then He stationed heavenly guards* at the east end of the garden of Eden and set up a sword of flames which guarded the tree of life on every side.

---

*I*n the measures between sin's arrival and the Liberating King's salvation many generations later, God never abandons His composition. He reveals His intentions piece-by-piece to our great ancestors such as Abraham, Sarah, Rebekah, Jacob, Joseph, Moses, Joshua, Deborah, David, Ezekiel, and Daniel. He writes them into the score so they can lead humanity away from sin's allure.

Moses is the ultimate example of God's chosen leader. We hear in the burning bush story how the Father responds to the pleas of His hurting children and moves to redeem them. He chooses Moses, a fugitive from Pharaoh's own household, and then reveals Himself to the reluctant prophet in the wilderness. Through a simple shepherd, God saves His people from slavery in Egypt and gives them a new covenant to live by. Moses is a wonderful leader, but he is only a man, and a flawed one at that. No matter how great he is, he can never liberate creation and return it to God's ideal; yet Moses' obedience foreshadows what is to come.

---

* 3:24 Literally *cherubim*

Exodus 3:1-15

¹When Moses was shepherding his father-in-law's flock (his father-in-law was Jethro, the priest of Midian), he guided the flock to the western side of the desert until he arrived at Horeb, which is God's mountain. ²There, the messenger of the Eternal One revealed himself to Moses in a fiery blaze from the center of a bush. Moses looked again at the bush as it blazed; and, to his amazement, the bush did not dissolve in the flames. *It was unhurt by the fire.*

| Moses | 3 | *(to himself)* How is it that the bush does not burn up in the fire? I need to move a little closer to find out the secret behind this mystery. |

⁴When the Eternal One saw Moses approach the burning bush to observe it more closely, He called out to him from within the bush.

| God | | Moses! Moses! |

Moses *was startled at the sound of the voice coming from within the bush.*

| Moses | | I'm right here. |

| God | 5 | Don't come any closer. Take your sandals off your feet, for the ground where you stand is holy. ⁶I am the True God, *the God* of your father, the God of Abraham, Isaac, and Jacob. |

A rush of dread and awe collapsed upon Moses, and he hid his face in fear of looking at the True God.

| God | *(continuing)* ⁷I have observed the misery of My people in Egypt. I have listened to their cries provoked by their cruel treatment, and I know all about their hardships and distress. ⁸I have come to rescue them from the authority of the Egyptians, to lead them from slavery and to give them a land—a wide, open space flowing with milk and honey. The land I have in mind is currently inhabited by Canaanites, Hittites, Amorites, Perizzites, Hivites, and Jebusites, *but with My help it will belong to the Israelites.* ⁹The plea of Israel's children has come before Me, and I have observed the cruel treatment they have suffered from Egyptian hands. ¹⁰So *leave behind the flocks and go back to Egypt.* I am appointing you as My messenger to the Pharaoh. I want you to be My voice, gather My people—the children of Israel—and bring them out of Egypt. |

¹¹*But Moses did not understand how he could be the one to fulfill such a destiny.*

Moses	11	*(to God)* Who am I that I should confront Pharaoh and lead Israel's children out of Egypt?
God	12	*Do not fear, Moses.* I will be with you, and this will be the sign to you that I am the One who has sent you: after you have led them out of Egypt, you will return to this mountain and worship the True God.
Moses	13	Let's say I go to the people of Israel and tell them, "The True God of your fathers has sent me to rescue you," and then they reply, "What is His name?" What should I tell them then?

God | 14 | I AM WHO I AM. This is what you should tell the people of Israel: "I AM has sent me to rescue you." ¹⁵This is what you are to tell Israel's people: "The Eternal God of your fathers, the God of Abraham, the God of Isaac, and the God of Jacob is the One who has sent me to you." This is My name forevermore, and this is the name by which all future generations shall remember Me.

*M*oses teaches us how to follow God's score by obeying His laws. But Moses' performance does not drown out the ever-present temptation to follow sin's off-beat rhythm. Moses plays a great part in liberating the Hebrew slaves and establishing the covenant. At times, he follows God perfectly, but sin's power proves too much even for him. Someone greater than Moses is needed to silence the dissonance and resolve our differences. From the beginning God knew that we needed a way to cover the disorder and harm that comes with sin. Not only are we punished for our sins, but we are also punished by our sins. The guilt, the stain, and the injury that comes from disobedience mount and eventually destroy. So He provides a way to deal with the scourge of sin: the way of sacrifice. In His covenant law with Israel, He prescribes ritual sacrifices. Those rituals performed in faith and repentance deal with some of the consequences of sin. But there is one event more than any that sets the tone for all future sacrifices. It is known as the Passover. These sacrifices model the greatest sacrifice that is to come when the Liberating King takes His place on the cross at Golgotha.

Exodus 12:21-28

²¹Then Moses gathered all of Israel's elders and gave them instructions.

Moses   Go and pick out the *sacrificial* lambs for your families, and then slaughter the Passover lamb. ²²Take a handful of hyssop and dip it into the blood-bowl. Mark the top of the doorway and the two doorposts with blood from the bowl. *After you do this,* no one should go outside the door of the house until *after the sun rises* the next morning.

²³The Eternal One will pass through *the land during the night* and death will invade *the homes of the sleeping* Egyptians. But when the Eternal One sees the blood-markings on the tops of the doorways and on the two doorposts, He will pass over your houses and not allow the agony of death to enter into your houses *while you watch through the night*. ²⁴You and all your descendants must observe this ritual *and teach these truths* for all times. ²⁵Even after you have arrived at the land the Eternal One has promised you—*the land flowing with rivers of milk and streams of honey*—you must still observe this ritual. ²⁶There will come a day when your children will ask you, "What does this ritual mean to you?" ²⁷You will answer them, "It is the Passover sacrifice to the Eternal One, who passed over the houses of Israel's sons and daughters *when we were slaves* in Egypt. The Eternal One allowed the agony of death to invade the homes of the *sleeping* Egyptians, but He spared our lives and our homes."

After this, the people bowed down and worshiped *the Eternal One.*
²⁸The Israelites went and did as they were instructed; they were obedient to what the Eternal One had commanded Moses and Aaron.

Section Two

The Composer and His Masterpiece
(A Child Has Been Born for Us)

*I*magine God taking a step back from His writing to admire the masterpiece He has created. He eyes the beauty of each orchestrated part; He feels the richness of each sound; the notes bounce to life as His sweet melody of redemption swells and weaves through His great composition.

While fine-tuning His work, He comes upon a section that sounds as if it doesn't belong. The percussion instruments have picked up a different beat; one section's rushing has unbalanced another's until the whole performance is off tempo. The Conductor begins to tap the stand as He realizes He's got to pull this piece back together under the original score before it crashes catastrophically. He enters the pit, gently reminds everyone to follow Him and attempts to draw those who are the source of the off-beat back into the enchanted pulse of the music.

Isn't this just like sin? It may start innocently enough with one player taking his or her eyes off God, but soon it infects those around us; and because it is easier to follow the populace and live distracted than to keep focused on God, lives are ruined. So God sends the Holy Spirit, the Conductor, to bring our lives, our voices, back into the chorus. He treasures this composition. A few rogue drums can't make God abandon His masterpiece and never perform it again. It will be performed with anyone who attends and follows His lead.

Even the strongest, purest human being cannot completely dissolve the dissonance of humanity. We can follow the minor human soloists for a while, people like Moses and David, but in the end no human can remedy the plague of the world. Only God Himself, the Great Healer, can cure us and completely, absolutely heal us from the disease of sin. Only the gift of the Liberating King can silence sin forever.

God (who has no beginning or end) makes His entrance to earth in human form as the Liberating King. Not only is the King's divinity important for our liberation, but it is a critical part of God's score that was composed before creation. Only God can properly perform the composition's climactic aria—redemption.

The Old Testament prophecies predict that the Liberating King will descend from David. As we will hear, the prophet Nathan instructs King David about God's plan to establish his dynasty as an eternal dynasty over Israel and Judah. How could David imagine that God had an even bigger role for him in the drama of redemption? God's promise to David becomes the basis for the expectation that one day the Liberating King will arrive.

In biblical times, genealogies functioned in a number of ways; one important way was political. It is important to show how the Liberating King descends from David because His genealogy gives Him the right to rule Israel and fulfill the Old Testament prophecies. His descent from David is recorded twice in extensive genealogies: Matthew begins with Abraham and records His ancestors through Joseph; and Luke traces His ancestry back to Adam through Mary. Joseph is included in both accounts because lineages ran from father to son, even though Joseph was not His blood relation.

In addition to revealing His identity, the prophecies tell of the nature, personality, and mission of the coming Liberating King. They also foreshadow circumstances and events that signal His arrival, provide a checklist to disprove false prophets, and give hope to hopeless people. The knowledge of a future liberation encourages everyone to follow the Composer during the centuries of despair between the fall of Jerusalem and the Liberating King's arrival.

But centuries of waiting influence the Jews' expectations of the heir of King David. They expect Him to be David-like—wealthy, handsome, strong, and politically powerful—not common and without any political standing. In the humblest of places, surrounded by the humblest of people, God arrives in the world through a woman as a vulnerable baby boy. Through Eve, and then Adam, people are separated from God. Yet God chooses an extraordinary woman to give birth to His Son. What does this tell us? It tells us that Eve shut the door to God, and Mary reopened it.

The story of the Liberating King—His birth, His life, and His death—is the sweet melody playing throughout Scripture. He arrives in a humble setting surrounded by humble creatures. He is visited by humble shepherds. He lives most of His life as a humble carpenter; and when He steps into public life, He spends time with humble fishermen and even a tax collector. He loves the unlovable—lepers, prostitutes, and riffraff. No wonder only a few believe this man is the Liberating King! If their expectation of the Liberator is a David-like warrior king, then they must be baffled by such a humble servant.

In our oratorio, the melody does not reveal itself in loud staccato passages; He is not announced by blaring trumpets and rhythmic marches. Rather, the melody slowly grows in rhythm and in volume as He is revealed to be the Liberating King.

Centuries before the Liberating King enters our world to liberate us from the powers of sin and death, God prepares the world with a word. His word, spoken through prophets and prophetesses, begins to reshape creation and prepares us to recognize and follow Him. So who can be that Liberating King? Who has the authority before God and among humans to silence the ever-present, hypnotizing counter-rhythm of sin? Such a leader must come from a strong family, so our Liberating King must have a genealogy that demands respect from kings and commoners and scholars. The greatest family in Israel is the family of King David—and our Liberating King descends from him.

Just as Moses leads Israel from slavery through the desert to the edge of the land of promise, so David takes the lead during the measures of the composition that establish Israel's united monarchy. He brings all twelve tribes of Israel under one government. He calls the nation back to follow the one God who called them to be a special people. Solidifying his rule, David desires to build a house, a temple for God in Jerusalem. Instead, God promises to provide a house—a family line through David culminating with the birth of the Liberating King. Through this Liberating King, David's dynasty will last forever.

1 Chronicles 17:10b-13

God | **10ᵇ** *(to Nathan)* I, the Eternal One, will build a house for you, *instead of you building a house for Me.* ¹¹⁻¹²At the end of your life, when your reign *on earth* is complete and you have joined your ancestors, I shall select one of your sons and I shall build his house. *This house will represent My authority over My people in Israel, and it will be the continuation of your dynasty. In return,* he will build a house for Me, *a temple where I shall dwell and where your people will worship Me.* And I will establish his throne forever. ¹³I shall be his Father, and he will be My son. I shall not take My favor from him as I took it from *Saul* who reigned before you. [14]I shall establish him *and his descendants as My representatives* in My temple and in My kingdom forever. His throne will last forever.

[15]Nathan told David exactly what the Eternal One said.

---

*I*n spite of God's great promise that David's descendants will rule forever, not all of the future kings follow the Conductor's lead. Some of David's sons remain distracted by sin. King Ahaz of Judah is one of the worst offenders, worshiping foreign gods and forming political alliances with foreign kings to try to insure the Southern Kingdom's safety. But despite Ahaz's many failures, it is within God's plan to move and save the nation from its enemies. So He sends Isaiah with a message to the fledgling players—a child will be born, a sign of God's saving grace; and before the boy knows right from wrong, the enemies of Ahaz will be destroyed. Well, it happened just as Isaiah said. God moved to save His people in that day, not by political power but by the sweet breath of a child. But this episode was not the climax of God's covenant. It was a sign of things to come.

Isaiah 7:11-13

| Eternal One | 11 | *(to Ahaz)* Ask for *proof,* a sign from your Eternal God—*Go ahead*, ask anything, anything at all. |
| Ahaz | 12 | No way. I wouldn't dare to ask, to test the Eternal One. |

Isaiah | **13**   *Don't be ridiculous! You are none other than* the House of David, *the one who inherited God's promise of perma-nent kingship for David's descendants.* Is it so easy to be a bore to people that you would exhaust God's patience, too? [14]*Suit yourself.* The Lord will give you a proof-sign, a pledge, anyway: See, a young maiden* will conceive. She will give birth to a son and name Him Immanuel, *that is, "God with us."* [15]*There will indeed be something Godlike about Him.* He'll choose what is right and good (rejecting what's not), and *prosperity will follow* as milk and honey flow once again.

Isaiah 9:6-7

[6]*Hope of all hopes, dream of our dreams,*
     a child has been born, *sweet-breathed,*
     a son is given to us: a living gift.
And even now, with tiny features and dewy hair,
     He is great. The power of leadership
     and the weight of authority
     will rest on His shoulders.
His name? His name
     we'll know in many ways—
He will be called Wonderful Counselor, *wise beyond belief,*
     the Great God,
Dear Father everlasting, ever-present never-failing,
     Master of wholeness,
     SarShalom (*which means* "Prince of peace").

---

* 7:14 LXX *virgin*

⁷His leadership will bring such prosperity *as you've never seen before —*
sustainable in its integrity, peace for all time.
This child will keep alive God's promise to David —
A throne forever, *right here among us.*
He will restore sound leadership
that will not, that cannot be perverted or shaken.
He will ensure justice without fail and absolute equity.
Always.
And if you are wondering: how will it happen?
The Eternal One, Commander of thousands, is driving
all the stars, furies, fates, and destinies toward its realization.
His passion is unstoppable.

In the measures between the prophecy and the arrival of the Liberating King, the people's anxiety grows as Jerusalem is destroyed, David's "eternal" dynasty appears to end, and God's covenant people are exiled. But even in exile, God cares for His wayward people and raises up a Persian king, Cyrus, to make a way for the people to return to their ancestral lands. Despite what seems to be good news, the Jewish people (as we know them today) rebuild a vassal state under ever-changing empires. With all their political problems, the Jews who heard the prophecies think they know what kind of leader the Liberating King should be. They expect His entrance onto the world stage to be announced by resounding trumpets! The anticipation of His political prowess is obvious in the negative reaction of King Herod (the Roman Empire's puppet-king of Judea). He orders the death of all male children who fit the prophets' descriptions, fearing the Liberator will overthrow his government. Herod's disharmony fills Judea with the sound of terror.

But some come to hear the prophecies differently. They are attuned to another reality where power looks like weakness and authority looks like service. They did not arrive at these insights through normal channels; they were spiritually discerned products of revelation. Matthew hears the Liberator's hushed entrance—devoid of trumpets and fanfare—he recognizes how Jesus fulfills the sign of the virgin birth and many other prophecies, and he proclaims His unusual birth as honorable. The child is so honorable, in fact, that sages from the east bring Him extravagant gifts, celebrating His birth and foreshadowing His role as the Liberating King. This soft melody drowns out false expectations and silences sin's rhythms.

Matthew 1:18-2:23

[18]So here, *finally*, is the story of the Liberator's birth *(it is quite a remarkable story)*:

Mary was engaged to marry Joseph, *son of David*. They hadn't married. And yet, some time well before their wedding date, Mary learned that she was pregnant by the Holy Spirit. [19]Joseph, because he was kind and upstanding and honorable, wanted to spare Mary shame. He did not wish to cause her more embarrassment than necessary.

[20]Now when Joseph had decided to act on his instincts, a messenger of the Lord came to him in a dream.

Messenger of the Lord	Joseph, son of David, do not be afraid to wed Mary and *bring her into your home and family* as your wife. *She did not sneak off and sleep with someone else*—rather,

she conceived the baby she now carries through the miraculous wonderworking of the Holy Spirit. ²¹She will have a Son, and you will name Him Jesus, *which means "the Lord saves,"* because this Jesus is the person who will save all of His people from sin.

²⁴Joseph woke up from his dream and did exactly what the messenger had told him to do: he married Mary and brought her into his home as his wife ²⁵(though he did not consummate their marriage until after her Son was born). *And when the baby was born,* Joseph named Him Jesus, *Savior.*[*]

²²*This is a remarkable and strange story. But it is not wholly surprising because years and years ago, Isaiah,* a prophet of Israel, foretold the story of Mary, Joseph, and Jesus.

Isaiah | 23   A virgin will conceive and bear a Son, and His name will be Immanuel (which is a Hebrew name that means "God with us").[*]

Matthew 2

¹Jesus was born in the town of Bethlehem, in the province of Judea, at the time when King Herod reigned. *Not long after Jesus was born,* magi, wise men or seers from the East, *understood that the One who would save His people from sin had been born, so they set off to find the baby Savior.* Making their way from the East to Jerusalem, these wise men asked, ²"Where is this newborn, who is the King of the Jews? When we

---

[*] 1:25 Verses 24 and 25 have been moved before verse 22 to help the reader understand the continuity of the passage.
[*] 1:23 Isaiah 7:14

were far away in the East we saw His star, and we have followed its glisten and gleam all this way to worship Him."

³King Herod began to hear rumors of the wise men's quest, and he, and all of his followers in Jerusalem, were worried. ⁴So Herod called all of the leading Jewish teachers, the chief priests and head scribes, and he asked them where *Hebrew tradition claimed* the long-awaited Liberator would be born.

Scribes and Priests	5	*An ancient Hebrew* prophet, *Micah*, said this: ⁶"But you, Bethlehem, in the land of Judah, are no poor relation— for from your people will come a Ruler who will be the shepherd of My people Israel."*

⁷Herod called the wise men to him, demanding to know the exact time the special star had appeared to them. ⁸Then Herod sent them to Bethlehem.

Herod	Go *to Bethlehem* and search high and low for this *Savior* child, and as soon as you know where He is, report it to me, so I may go and worship Him.

⁹⁻¹⁰The wise men *left Herod's chambers* and went on their way. The star they had first seen in the East reappeared—a miracle that, of course, overjoyed and enraptured the wise men. The star led them to the house where Jesus lay, ¹¹and as soon as the wise men arrived, they saw Him with His mother Mary, and they bowed down and worshiped Him. They unpacked their satchels and gave Jesus gifts of gold, frankincense, and myrrh.

¹²And then, *just as Joseph did a few months before*, the wise men had a dream warning them not to go back to Herod. *The wise men*

* 2:6 Micah 5:2

heeded the dream. Ignoring Herod's instructions, they returned to their homes in the East by a different route.

¹³After the wise men left, a messenger of the Lord appeared to Joseph in a dream.

Messenger of the Lord	*(to Joseph)* Get up, take the child and His mother, and head to Egypt. Stay there until I tell you *it is safe to leave*. For Herod *understands that Jesus threatens him and all he stands for.* He is planning to search for the child and kill Him. *But you will be safe in Egypt.*

¹⁴So Joseph got up in the middle of the night; he bundled up Mary and Jesus, and they left for Egypt.*

¹⁶*After a few months had passed*, Herod realized he'd been tricked. The wise men *were not coming back; they weren't going to lead him to the infant King*. Herod, *of course*, was furious, *but he was not to be out-done*. He simply ordered that all boys who lived in or near Bethlehem and were two years of age and younger be killed. *He knew the baby King was this age* because of what the wise men told him.

¹⁷This *sad event* had long been foretold by the prophet Jeremiah:

Jeremiah	18	A voice will be heard in Ramah, weeping *and wailing* and mourning *out loud all day and night.* The voice is Rachel's, weeping for her children, her children who have been killed; she weeps, and she will not be comforted.*

---

* 2:14 Verse 15 has been moved to follow verse 18 to help the reader understand the continuity of the passage.
* 2:18 Jeremiah 31:15

¹⁵Joseph, Mary, and Jesus *stayed in Egypt* until Herod died. This fulfilled yet another prophecy. The prophet *Hosea* once wrote, "Out of Egypt I called My Son."*

¹⁹And after Herod died, a messenger of the Lord appeared in a dream to Joseph in Egypt:

Messenger	20	*You may go home now.* Take the child and His mother
of the		and go back to the land of Israel, for the people who
Lord		were trying to take the child's life are now dead.

²¹So Joseph got up and took Mary and Jesus and returned to the land of Israel. ²²Soon he learned that Archelaus, Herod's *oldest and notoriously brutal son,* was ruling Judea. *Archelaus, Joseph knew, might not be any friendlier to Joseph and his family than Herod had been.* Joseph was simply afraid. *He had another dream, and* in this dream, he was warned *away from Judea;* so Joseph *decided* to settle *up north in a district called* Galilee, ²³in a town called Nazareth. And this, too, fulfilled what the prophets have taught, *"The Savior* will be a Nazarene."*

---

ot only is the birth of Jesus, the Liberating King, recognized by the wise men from the East, but it is also acknowledged by some commoners—the very kind people who later become His entourage. Surrounded by a concert of chaos, these poor shepherds are treated to a festival of heavenly glory and an angelic chorus announcing the birth of a different sort of king. Their ears are tuned to the sweet melody of an infant Liberator in humble surroundings. The infant Jesus appeals to the shepherds because He comes from

---

* 2:15 Hosea 11:1
* 2:23 Judges 13:5; Isaiah 11:1

common beginnings: His father is a simple carpenter, and His mother is young and innocent. In spite of His royal heritage, He does not have the benefit of earthly wealth or political power, and these commoners are the first to recognize Him.

Luke 2:8-19

[8]Nearby, in the fields outside of Bethlehem, a group of shepherds were guarding their flocks *from predators* in the darkness of night. [9]Suddenly, a messenger of the Lord stood in front of them, and the darkness was replaced by a glorious light—the shining light of God's glory. They were terrified!

Messenger | 10 | Don't be afraid! Listen! I bring good news, news of great joy, news that will affect all people everywhere. [11]Today, in the city of David, a Liberator has been born for you! He is the promised Liberating King, the Supreme Authority! [12]You will know you have found Him when you see a baby, wrapped in a blanket, lying in a feeding trough.

[13]At that moment, the first heavenly messenger was joined by thousands of other messengers—a vast heavenly choir. They praised God.

Heavenly Choir | 14 | To the highest heights of the universe, glory to God! And on earth, peace among all people who bring pleasure to God!

[15]As soon as the heavenly messengers disappeared into heaven, the shepherds were buzzing with conversation.

| Shepherds | Let's rush down to Bethlehem right now! Let's see what's happening! Let's experience what the Lord has told us about! |

[16]So they ran into town, and *eventually* they found Mary and Joseph and the baby lying in the feeding trough. After they saw the baby, [17]they spread the story of *what they had experienced and* what had been said to them about this child. [18]Everyone who heard their story couldn't stop thinking about its meaning. [19]Mary too pondered all of these events, treasuring each memory in her heart.

The Liberating King has arrived, and He is recognized by wise foreigners and common shepherds alike. But what about the religious scholars—the ones who know the prophecies? Shouldn't they welcome Him too? In spite of their training, or maybe because of it, many of them do not see beyond their partial hopes. They know the resume of the king they want—a king wielding the same kind of power that had subdued them for nearly five centuries.

More than 30 years after His miraculous birth, Jesus steps onto the stage of world history and proclaims in elegant tones the mystery of God's coming kingdom. Many religious scholars, however, are not satisfied that Jesus is indeed the Liberating King. Despite everything Jesus does and says, they refuse to recognize Him as God's chosen. Jesus may descend from David—they don't argue that—but so do some of them. For reasons only they know, He doesn't command their respect. He has authority, at least according to the thousands of common people who come to hear and see Him, but what do they know? They have no training. They have no power. So opponents come from all sides, from every party and special interest, to challenge His teaching and question His honor. One day Jesus uses their own Scriptures to pose a riddle.

Matthew 22:41-46

[41]Since the Pharisees were gathered together there, Jesus *took the opportunity to* pose a question of His own.

Jesus	42	What do you think about the Liberating King, *the Anointed One? Whose Son is He?*
Pharisees		*But, of course,* He is the Son of David.
Jesus	43	Then how is it that David—*whose words were surely shaped* by the Spirit—calls Him "Lord"? [44]*For in his Psalms—or perhaps you haven't opened your psalter recently—*David writes,

> "The Lord said to my lord
>   'Sit here at My right hand,
>   *in the place of honor and power,*
> And I will gather Your enemies together,
>   *lead them in on hands and knees,*
>   and You will rest Your feet on their backs.'"*

	45	How can David call his own Son "Lord"?

[46]No one had an answer to Jesus' question. And from that day forward, no one asked Him anything.

* 22:44 Psalm 110:1

Section Three

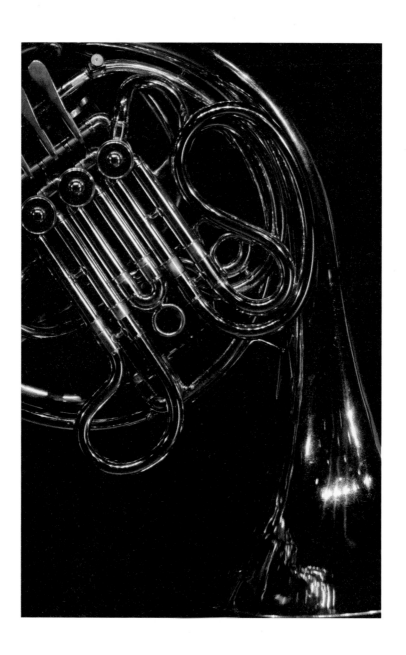

Melody of the Ages
(Perfectly Fitted)

The melody of the ages contained in the Bible says little about the childhood of Jesus. What was it like for Jesus to grow up? What were His first words? Did He ever get into mischief? Did He struggle with His self-image? When did He first know who He was and what He came to do? Many of us wonder about such questions at some point during our journey because we have mixed feelings about our own childhood and awkward adolescence. We remember the good times (family vacations, neighborhood adventures with friends, first kisses, magical summers), but we also remember the difficult times (fights with our friends, broken hearts, and home-sickness). How different must it have been for Jesus? He experienced all of our temptations, but He never fell into them.

One of the few stories of Jesus' childhood tells us a lot about His mind-set at the awkward age of 12. Every year He and His parents journey to Jerusalem for the Passover. This is a pilgrimage festival, not at all like our family vacations. The destination is Jerusalem, the holiest city on earth, and the temple, the holiest place on earth.

It's hard for us to imagine what it must have been like gazing up from the streets at the temple as it rose high into the sky. This is the one place on earth where heaven and earth meet, the one place God promises always to turn a listening ear. Pilgrims travel together, in large extended families and communities, to commemorate the Passover. Of all the feasts that God ordained, this is everyone's favorite because it celebrates how God liberated the Hebrew slaves from the cruel hands and even crueler whips of the Egyptians. But on this trip, it is what happened after the Passover that attracts everyone's attention.

As Jesus' parents are on their way back home from the feast, they realize He is not with them in the caravan of traveling pilgrims. They return to Jerusalem; and after three days of looking for Jesus, they finally find Him in the temple sitting among the teachers, listening and challenging them with questions.

Luke tells us of the witnesses' reaction to this scene: "Everyone was surprised and impressed that a 12-year-old boy could have such deep understanding and could answer questions *with such wisdom*."[4] When Mary and Joseph ask Jesus why He would worry His parents by wandering off, He replies: "Why did you need to look for Me? Didn't you know that I must be working for My Father?"[5] Although Jesus is only 12, He must already know He is very special. Unfortunately, stories about His childhood end here.

The Liberator's story picks up about 18 years later when Jesus learns that His cousin, John, is preaching in the wilderness about returning to God. Something stirs in Him, so Jesus leaves behind the carpenter shop in Galilee for the Judean desert. When He arrives at the Jordan River several days later, He sees John surrounded by disciples. He hears John's message about God's coming kingdom. He knows that His time has come. So John immerses Jesus in the gentle, running water of the Jordan to fulfill God's righteousness, and the Spirit of God descends upon Jesus. At that time, Jesus receives the ultimate validation of His identity when the heavens open and God declares Him the Liberating King.

The same Spirit that falls on Jesus at the Jordan River drives Him into the desert. There He fasts and prays for 40 days. Deep into the fast, after the hunger returns, He faces three temptations from

[4] Luke 2:47
[5] Luke 2:49

the evil one who consistently strives to throw humanity off beat. Jesus meets each with quiet dignity and Scripture. When Jesus returns from the desert, He begins His public ministry, performing miracles, teaching the masses, calling disciples, and revealing His authority as the Liberating King.

*L*ong before Jesus left His carpenter's shop in Nazareth for public life, the prophets heard the voice of the Lord. The message had a clear and unmistakable theme, repeated time and again so there could be no confusion. The Liberating King would not just arrive and reveal Himself to the world; He would be announced. A messenger, a prophet, would go before Him, give voice to God's message, and ready the world for His entrance. Like a blaring trumpet, he would command the attention of both great and small.

Malachi 3:1-3

¹These are the words of the Eternal One, the God of the heavenly armies:

Eternal One	Behold! I am sending My messenger,
	and he will clear the road ahead for Me.
	The Lord you seek will suddenly arrive at His temple
	and the messenger of God's covenant, your soul's delight.
	Watch! Because He too is coming.

2   Can anyone live through the day when He arrives?
        Will anyone be left standing when He appears?

He is a purifying fire;
> He is lye soap.
3 Like a refiner of silver,
> He will purify the descendants of Levi—
> until they are pure, unalloyed gold and silver.
Then they *will draw near to* the Eternal One,
> presenting offerings with righteous, *clean hands*.

John the wandering prophet is that lone voice, the trumpet announcing the arrival of God's great and glorious kingdom. He is the Elijah-like prophet promised centuries earlier who will ready the world for the Liberating King. But even John has questions and doubts. As Jesus travels in Galilee healing and teaching, John is imprisoned. He is regarded as an irritant by a rather irritating man who happens to be the governor. Is this his destiny—to rot, or worse, to lose his head in some political appointee's prison? Is this what he signed on for? Or has he been wrong about Jesus? How can this be God's rule? So John summons his followers to his cell and sends them to Jesus with a question: "Are You the One, or should we look for another?" Jesus answers John's reasonable question gently with Scripture; He knows what happens to every prophet who dares to confront evil. But the record is silent on how the imprisoned prophet takes it. In only a few days, Herod will claim his head.

Despite John's doubts, Jesus counts John as one of the greatest people in history. His life spans two covenants. He is the hinge between the old age and the new.

Matthew 11:1-30

[1]With that, Jesus finished instructing His disciples, and He went on to preach and teach in the towns *of Galilee*. [2]John the Teacher who dipped people, meanwhile, was still in prison. But stories about the Liberating King's teachings and healing reached him.

So John sent his followers [3]to question Jesus.

John's Followers	Are You the One we have been expecting as Savior for so long? *Are You the One Scripture promised would come?* Or should we expect someone else?
Jesus 4	Go back and tell John the things you have heard and the things you have seen. [5]*Tell him you have seen* the blind receive sight, the lame walk, the lepers cured, the deaf hear, the dead raised, and the good news preached to the poor. [6]Blessed are those who *understand what is afoot and* stay on My narrow path.

[7]John's disciples left, and Jesus began to speak to a crowd about John. *He wanted to make sure people understood who they had seen when they saw John.*

Jesus	What did you go into the desert to see? Did you expect to see a reed blowing around in the wind? [8]No? Were you expecting to see a man dressed in the finest silks? No, of course not—you find silk in the sitting rooms of palaces and mansions, not in the middle of the wilderness. [9]So what did you go out to see? A prophet? Yes. Yes, a prophet and more than a prophet. [10]When you

saw John, you saw the one whom the prophet *Malachi envisioned when he* said, "I will send My messenger ahead of You, and he will prepare the way for You."*

[11]This is the truth: no one who has ever been born to a woman is greater than John the Immersing Teacher.* And yet the most insignificant person in the kingdom of heaven is greater than he. [12-13]All of the prophets of old, all of the law—that was all prophecy leading up to the coming of John. *Now, the time for that sort of prophecy is through. All of that prophecy and teaching was to prepare us to come to this very point, right here and now.* When John the Teacher* who ritually cleansed came, the kingdom of heaven began to break in upon us and those in power are trying to clamp down on it—*why do you think John is in jail?* [14]If only you could see it—John is the Elijah, the prophet we were promised would come *and prepare the way*. [15]He who has ears *for the truth*, let him hear.

[16]What is this generation like? You are like children sitting in the marketplace and calling out, [17]"When we played the flute, you did not dance; and when we sang a dirge, you did not mourn." [18]*What I mean is this:* When John came, *he came from a place of the wilderness. He dressed in the clothes of an outcast, and* he did not eat but lived on honey and wild locusts. And people wondered *if he was crazy*, if he had been possessed by a demon. [19]Then the Son of Man appeared—He didn't fast, as John had, but ate *with sinners* and drank *wine.*

---

* 11:10 Malachi 3:1
* 11:11 Literally, John who immersed, to show repentance
* 11:12-13 Literally, John who immersed, to show repentance

And the people said, "This man is a glutton! He's a drunk! And He hangs around with tax collectors and sinners, to boot." Well, Wisdom will be vindicated by her actions—*not by your opinions*.

²⁰Then Jesus began to preach about the towns He'd visited. He'd performed some of His most fantastic miracles *in places like Chorazin and Bethsaida*, but still the people in those places hadn't turned to God.

Jesus | **21** Woe to you, Chorazin! And woe to you, Bethsaida! Had I gone to Tyre and Sidon and performed miracles there, they would have repented immediately, taking on sackcloth and ashes. ²²But I tell you this: the people from Tyre and Sidon will fare better on the day of judgment than you will. ²³And Capernaum! Do you think you will reign exalted in heaven? *No*, you'll rot in hell. Had I gone to Sodom and worked miracles there, *the people would have repented, and* Sodom would still be standing, *thriving, bustling.* ²⁴*Well, you know what happened to Sodom.* But know this—the people from Sodom will fare better on the day of judgment than you will.

²⁵And then Jesus began to pray:

Jesus I praise You, Father—Lord of heaven and earth. You have revealed Your truths to the lowly *and the ignorant, the children and the crippled, the lame and the mute.* You have hidden wisdom from those who pride themselves on being so wise and learned. ²⁶You did this, simply, because it pleased You. ²⁷The Father has handed over everything to My care. No one knows the Son except the Father, and no one knows the Father except the Son—and those to whom the Son wishes to reveal the Father. ²⁸Come to Me, all who are weary and burdened, and I will give you rest. ²⁹Put My yoke upon your shoulders—*it might appear heavy at first, but it is perfectly fitted to your curves.* Learn from Me, for I am gentle and humble of heart. *When you are yoked to Me, your weary souls will find rest.* ³⁰For My yoke is easy, and My burden is light.

The gentle carpenter from Nazareth soon becomes a polarizing figure. People could not hear His message and remain neutral. He does not give His followers that option; He demands that they hear Him and follow Him. Some follow, others choose early on to oppose His every move and to criticize His motives. Even though His following is growing, many people remain confused. Is He the prophet like Moses that Scripture says is coming? Is He the reincarnation of some prophet from the past? The people know there is something special about Him based on the authority in His teachings, His brilliantly woven parables, and His amazing miracles. Secretly, they hope He will be the one to lead them as Moses and David did before Him—but they do not yet realize He is their Liberating King.

Mark 8:27-29

²⁷As He traveled with His disciples into the villages of Caesarea Philippi, He posed an *important* question to them.

Jesus | Who are the people saying I am?

²⁸They told Him *about the great speculation in the land concerning His identity.*

Disciples		Some of them say John the Prophet,* others say Elijah, while others say one of the prophets of old.
Jesus	29	*(pressing the question)* And who do you say that I am?
Peter		You are the Liberating King, *God's Anointed One.*

> *P*eter has no way of knowing how right he is about Jesus. But in a few days, he will glimpse the true glory that is his Master's destiny. Jesus takes His inner circle up on a high mountain in Galilee where He is transfigured in their presence. In that mysterious moment, Peter, James, and John stand in awe and amazement as they realize the truth about the Liberating King. If they had any doubts about their answer to Jesus' question, "Who do you say that I am?" those doubts are erased by the transcendent, glorious light of the transfiguration. In that vision, God endorses His Son as the Liberating King.

Matthew 17:1-8

¹Six days later, Jesus went up to the top of a high mountain with Peter, James, and John. ²There, *something spectacular happened:* Jesus' face began to glow and gleam and shine like the morning sun. His clothes gleamed, too—bright white, like sunlight *mirroring off a snowfall.* He

---

* 8:28 the Immerser

was, *in a word,* transfigured. ³Suddenly there at the top of the mountain were Moses and Elijah, *those icons of the faith, beloved of God.* And they talked to Jesus. *The three men stood at the intersection of heaven and earth; they were gleaming, talking.*

Peter | 4 Lord, how amazing that we are here *to see these heroes of our faith, these men through whom God spoke.* Should I quickly build some shelter, three *small* tabernacles, for You, for Moses, and for Elijah?

⁵As Peter spoke, a bright cloud enveloped all of them.

Voice from the Cloud | This is My beloved Son. With Him I am well pleased. Listen to Him.

⁶This voice from heaven terrified the three disciples, and they fell prostrate on the ground. ⁷But Jesus—*who was, by this time, used to His disciples being plagued by fear*—touched them.

Jesus | Get up. Don't be afraid.

⁸And when the disciples got up, they saw they were alone with their Lord. *Moses and Elijah had returned from where they came.*

*I*t's ironic that in the Gospels the first "creatures" to recognize Jesus after His baptism are the demons. While teaching in Capernaum, demons identify Jesus as the Holy One of God and He rebukes them. But this exchange is not enough to convince doubters and skeptics of His status as the Liberating King. Instead, they charge that He is aligned with Satan because He wields power over the dark forces. Jesus pokes holes in their logic and claims instead to be in a full-frontal assault against the powers that appear to hold sway over the world. As He casts out demons, feeds the hungry, heals the sick, and calms the storms.

Luke 4:31-37

31-33Next He went to Capernaum, another Galilean city. Again He was *in the synagogue* teaching on the Sabbath, and as before, the people were enthralled by His words. He had a way of saying things—a special authority, *a unique power.*

In attendance that day was a man with a demonic spirit.

Demon-Possessed Man	34	*(screaming at Jesus) Get out of here!* Leave us alone! What's Your agenda, Jesus of Nazareth? Have You come to destroy us? I know who You are: You're the Holy One, the One sent by God!
Jesus	35	*(firmly rebuking the demon)* Be quiet. Get out of that man!

Then the demonic spirit immediately threw the man into a fit, and he collapsed right there in the middle of the synagogue. It was clear the demon had come out, and the man was completely fine after that. 36Everyone was shocked to see this, and they couldn't help but talk about it.

| Synagogue Members | What's this about? What's the meaning of this message? Jesus speaks with authority, and He has power to command demonic spirits to go away. |

[37]The excitement about Jesus spread into every corner of the surrounding region.

> ore than any other prophet, Isaiah seems to hear the music clearly and to know how the story of redemption will be resolved. When God called the Israelites to be His people, they were chosen for a purpose: to be a light to the nations. But this proved too difficult. They failed over and over again to live up to the gifts God had provided. Isaiah senses this in ways others do not. For him, it is not enough for the Liberating King to rescue Israel from exile and restore David's dynasty; the Liberator is the incarnation of God's glory and eclipses the darkness that governs the nations. He is the true Light that comes to illuminate the world.

Isaiah 60:1-3

[1]Arise, shine, for your light has broken through!
Stand and be a light yourself because your light has come.
The Eternal One's brilliance has dawned upon you.
[2]*See truly*; look *carefully*—darkness blankets the earth;
people all over *are living in a fog.*
But God will shine on you;
The Eternal One's bright glory will shine on you,
a light for all to see.

³Nations *north and south*, peoples *east and west*,
  will be drawn to your light,
  will find purpose and direction by your light.
In the radiance of your rising, you will enlighten the leaders of nations.

---

*O*ne of the first outsiders to recognize His true identity is a Samaritan woman. In a small town north of Jerusalem, Jesus sits by a well to talk with her. According to social customs of the day, Jesus should not interact with a woman, especially one from Samaria. Even more surprising is His offer of liberation to her; she is one of the first people invited to experience eternal life.

John 4:5-29

⁵⁻⁸In a *small* Samaritan town known as Sychar, Jesus *and His entourage* stopped to rest at the historic well that Jacob gave his son Joseph. It was about noon when Jesus found a spot to sit close to the well while the disciples ventured off to find provisions. *From His vantage He watched as* a Samaritan woman approached to draw some water. *Unexpectedly,* He spoke to her.

Jesus		Would you draw Me a drink?
Woman	9	I cannot believe that You, a Jew, would associate with me, a Samaritan woman, much less ask me to give You a drink.

Jews, you see, have no dealings with Samaritans. *Besides, a man would never approach a woman like this in public. Jesus was breaking accepted social barriers with this confrontation.*

Jesus	10	You don't know the gift of God or who is asking you for a drink *of this water from Jacob's well.* Because if you did, you would have asked Him *for something greater* and He would have given you the living water.
Woman	11	Sir, You sit by this deep well *a thirsty man* without a bucket in sight. Where does this living water come from? *Do You believe You can draw water and share it with me?* [12]Are You claiming superiority to our father Jacob who labored long and hard to dig *and maintain* this well so that he could share clean water with his sons, *grandchildren,* and cattle?
Jesus	13	Drink this water, and your thirst is quenched only for a moment. *You must return to this well again and again.* [14]I offer water that will become a wellspring within you that gives life throughout eternity. You will never be thirsty again.
Woman	15	*Please*, sir, give me some of this water, so I'll never be thirsty and never again have to make the trip to this well.
Jesus	16	Then bring your husband to Me.
Woman	17-18	I do not have a husband.
Jesus		Technically you are telling the truth. But you have had five husbands and are currently living with a man you are not married to.
Woman	19	Sir, it is obvious to me that You are a prophet. *Maybe You can explain to me why our peoples disagree about*

how to worship: ²⁰Our fathers worshiped here on this mountain, but Your people say that Jerusalem is the only place for all to worship. *Which is it?*

Jesus	21-24	Woman, I tell you that neither *is so*. Believe this: a new day is coming—in fact, it's already here—when the importance will not be placed on the time and place of worship but on the truthful hearts of worshipers. You worship what you don't know while we worship what we do know, for God's salvation is coming through the Jews. The Father is spirit, and He is seeking followers whose worship is sourced in truth and deeply spiritual as well. Regardless of whether you are in Jerusalem or on this mountain, if you do not seek the Father, then you do not worship.
Woman	25	These mysteries will be made clear by the coming Liberator, the Anointed One.
Jesus	26	The Liberating King speaks to you. I am the One you have been looking for.

²⁷The disciples returned to Him *and gathered around Him* in amazement that He would *openly break their customs by* speaking to this woman, but none of them would ask Him what He was looking for or why He was speaking with her. ²⁸The woman went back to the town, leaving her water pot behind. She stopped men *and women* on the streets and told them about what had happened.

Woman	29	*I met* a stranger who knew everything about me. Come and see for yourselves; can He be the Liberating King?

*W*hat fires the prophetic imagination? What can make prophets leave their rather calm, relatively mundane lives to speak for God under threats of ostracism and death? They hear the voice of God calling them to speak truth to the powerful and to leave comfort for affliction. When they obey, they suffer; so what motivates them to listen to the Voice? The sheer weight of hope. Hope keeps them, motivates them, and comforts them.

No prophet could hear the hopeful melody of redemption better than Isaiah. He saw things only a few had seen. He heard things only a few expected. He saw that God Himself would visit the dark, diseased, dry, and dangerous place we call home. Ultimately, what we know today—what Isaiah saw dimly—is that the coming of the Liberating King is the coming of God. He comes for justice and healing. He comes to water dry, desert places. He comes to establish a peaceable kingdom and to end the punishing exile. He comes to exchange our sadness for His joy.

Isaiah 35:4-10

⁴Tell those who worry, the anxious *and fearful*,
  "Take strength; have courage! *There's nothing to fear.*
  Look, here—your God! Right here is your God!
The balance is shifting;
  God is setting to rights.
  None other than God will give you success.
He is coming to make you safe."

⁵Then, *such healing, such repair:*
  the eyes of the blind will be opened,
  the ears of the deaf will be clear *to hear the ring of music.*

⁶The lame will leap like deer *excited*;
>   *they will run and jump tirelessly and gracefully*.
> *The stutterer, the stammerer,* and the tongue of the mute
>   will sing out loud and strong, *clear as a new day*.
⁷Water will pour through the deserts;
>   the godforsaken lands will drink deep draughts.
>   *Hardened wastelands will shimmer with life.*
>   *Abandoned villages* where predators lurked
>   will be grassy playgrounds.
> Dry land will turn lush and green.

⁸And the road to this happy renovation will be clearly signed.
>   People will declare the way itself to be holy—the route, "sacred."
> Only those who are right with God
>   will be able to walk its pleasant path,
> And nobody, no visitor, no dimwit, will get lost along it.
⁹There'll be no lions lying in wait,
>   no predators or dangers in sight.
>   Only those made right with God will journey there.
¹⁰Those whom the Eternal One has recalled from a punishing exile,
>   they will go along so easily.
>   They will walk this path,
> Come waltzing to Zion, singing their way
>   *to that place of right relation to God*.
> An aura of joy never-ending will attend them;
>   they will clasp gladness and joy to their hearts,
> while sadness and despair evaporate into thin air.

The Scriptures are clear. When the Liberating King arrives, He will repair the world through miracles, the likes of which have never been seen before. He will raise the dead and heal those who've been sick all their lives. But Jesus' miracles are not always what they seem. When encountering a crippled man, Jesus' first concern is for his spiritual liberation, not his physical freedom. He uses the opportunity to demonstrate who He is and the priorities of the Kingdom.

Jesus knew what we've forgotten. Maybe it was part of our hardwiring as human beings made in God's image and likeness. Somewhere we got the idea that our greatest need is for physical healing. Jesus, however, knew what was in the soul of man. On this occasion, He looked past the obvious—the man's crippling paralysis—to perform the greatest miracle of all: the forgiveness of sins.

Luke 7:11-17

¹¹It wasn't long after this when Jesus entered a city called Nain. Again all of His disciples accompanied Him, along with a huge crowd. ¹²He was coming near the gate of the city as a corpse was being carried out. This man was the only child *and support* of his widowed mother, and she was accompanied by a large funeral crowd.

¹³As soon as the Lord saw her, He felt compassion for her.

Jesus | Don't weep.

¹⁴Then He came to the stretcher, and those carrying it stood still.

Jesus | Young man, listen! Get up!

¹⁵The dead man immediately sat up and began talking. Jesus presented him to his mother, ¹⁶and everyone was both shocked and jubilant. They praised God.

| Funeral Crowd | A tremendous prophet has arisen in our midst! God has visited His people! |

¹⁷News of Jesus spread across the whole province of Judea and beyond to the surrounding regions.

Luke 5:17-26

¹⁷One day Jesus was teaching *in a house*, and the healing power of the Lord was with Him. Pharisees and religious scholars were sitting and listening, having come from villages all across the regions of Galilee and Judea and from *the holy city* of Jerusalem.

¹⁸Some men came *to the house*, carrying a paralyzed man on his bed pallet. They wanted to bring him in and present him to Jesus, ¹⁹but the house was so packed with people that they couldn't get in. So they climbed up on the roof and pulled off some roof tiles. Then they lowered the man *by ropes* so he came to rest right in front of Jesus.

²⁰In this way, their faith was visible to Jesus.

| Jesus | *(to the man on the pallet)* My friend, all your sins are forgiven. |

²¹The Pharisees and religious scholars were offended at this. They turned to one another and asked questions.

| Pharisees and Religious Scholars | Who does He think He is? Wasn't that blasphemous? Who can pronounce that a person's sins are forgiven? Who but God alone? |

| Jesus | 22 | *(responding with His own question)* Why are your hearts full of questions? [23]Which is easier to say, "Your sins are forgiven," or, "Get up and walk"? [24]Just so you'll know that the Son of Man is fully authorized to forgive sins on earth (He turned to the paralyzed fellow lying on the stretcher), I say, get up, take your mat, and go home. |

[25]Then, right in front of their eyes, the man stood up, picked up his bed, and left to go home—full of praises for God! [26]Everyone was stunned. They couldn't help but feel awestruck, and they praised God too.

| People | We've seen extraordinary things today. |

Section Four

The Orchestra Waits with Anticipation (He Will Feed His Fold)

*I*t is midnight. A deep silence blankets the earth. Stars pierce the darkness. A flock of sheep huddle together in a nearby field. A shepherd sits on a rock not far away, fighting sleep but maintaining a watchful eye. But one mischievous young lamb has strayed and lies asleep behind a rock on a nearby hill.

There's a frightful noise. The lamb awakens to the low growl of a wolf coming from the other side of the rock. The lamb cannot move—it is paralyzed with fear. The wolf shrieks; then there's silence. The lamb hooks his neck nervously around the rock, and standing there is the shepherd, its protector, who has killed the wolf and saved the lamb's life.

We are that mischievous lamb, and the Lord is our shepherd. He guides us through the meadows of life and protects us from the dangers that lurk at night. And, as long as we are not too far away from Him, He can clamp down on the snapping jaws of evil.

When Jesus calls Himself "the good shepherd," His disciples hear the echo of Psalm 23, "The Eternal One is my shepherd. . . ." But despite our romantic notions to the contrary, shepherding was not a noble profession in those days. So why would God choose to reveal Himself as a shepherd? It is because we are more like sheep than we'd like to admit and because He has committed Himself to serve, protect, and provide for us.

> I am the good shepherd. The good shepherd lays down His life for the sheep *in His care*. The hired hand is not like the shepherd caring for His own sheep. When a wolf attacks,

snatching and scattering the sheep, he runs for his life, leaving them *defenseless*. The hired hand runs because he works only for wages and does not care for the sheep. I am the good shepherd; I know My sheep, and My sheep know Me. As the Father knows Me, I know the Father; I will give My life for the sheep.[6]

Just as a true shepherd knows each one of his sheep by name, God knows every one of us. And, just as every sheep's life is important to a shepherd, so ours are important to the Good Shepherd.

Isaiah 40:1-5, 11

[1]"Comfort, comfort My people," says your God.
　　[2]"With the gentlest words, *tender and kind*,
Assure this city, this site of long-ago chosenness; speak unto Jerusalem
　　their battles are over. The terror, the bloodshed, the horror
　　of My punishing work is done.
This place has paid for its guilt; iniquity is pardoned;
　　its term of incarceration is complete.
　　It has endured double the punishment it was due."

[3]A voice is wailing, "In the wilderness,
　　get it ready! Prepare the way,
　　make it a straight shot. The Eternal One would have it so.
Straighten the way in the wandering desert
　　to make the crooked road wide and straight for our God.

[6] John 10:11-15

⁴Where there are steep valleys, treacherous descents, raise the highway,
    lift it up;
    bring down the dizzying heights; humble them.
Fill the potholes and gullies, the rough places.
    Iron out the shoulders flat and wide.
⁵The Eternal One will be, really be, among us.
    The radiant glory *of the Lord* will be revealed.
    All flesh together will take it in.
    Believe it. None other than God, the Eternal One has spoken."

¹¹He will feed His fold like a shepherd;
    God will assure that we are safe and content.
He will gather together His lambs, *the weak and the wobbly ones*
    into His arms,
    carrying them close to His bosom.
And God tenderly leads those *burdened by care-taking*
    Like a shepherd leads the mothers of her lambs.

A recurring theme throughout Scripture is the ideal image that God relates to His people as a shepherd to his sheep. After the conquest of Jerusalem by the Babylonians, prophets and poets described God as the ultimate shepherd—guarding, providing, protecting, leading, and eventually herding His flock back to a New Jerusalem.

But the shepherd image can cut both ways. Israel and Judah often suffered exploitation and harm at the hands of wayward shepherds, harsh leaders more concerned about themselves than about their flock. But in Israel's critical moments, God's prophets envisioned another shepherd striding forward, Jesus our Liberating King. He would do more than shepherd us during this life; He would shepherd us for all the ages to come. And where would David's Son learn to shepherd us? From His Father and our God. The Lord is our shepherd.

Ezekiel 34:11-24

¹¹This is what the Lord, the Eternal One, says:

Eternal One

I will personally go out searching for My sheep. I will find them wherever they are, *and I will look after them.* ¹²In the same way that a shepherd seeks after, *cares for, and watches over* his scattered flock, so will I be the guardian of My congregation. I will be their Rescuer! *No matter where they have scattered, I will journey to find them.* I will bring them back from the places where they were scattered on that dark and cloudy day. *I will reach into hard-to-reach places; I will search out every secret pocket of the earth in order to save them from the darkness.* ¹³⁻¹⁴I will call them out from the nations and gather them from the countries, and I will bring them into their own land. I will give them *a sanctuary—a place where they can rest*—in the high mountain pastures and meadows of Israel. The mountain heights of Israel will be their nourishment, *their sanctuary.* I will introduce them to blooming pastures, where they can graze upon rich mountain lands *to* soothe their hunger. I will lead them along the banks of *glistening mountain* streams, *where they can drink clear, pure water and quench their thirst.*

¹⁵I will *watch over My sheep and* feed My flock. *Whenever they are tired*, they can lie down in the cool, *mountain grass* and rest *for as long as they like.* ¹⁶When they are lost, I will look for them and bring back every last stray. I will bind up the injured and strengthen the weak. However, I will make sure the fat and powerful *do not take advantage of the others*. I will feed them a healthy portion of judgment.

¹⁷As for you, my flock, this is what the Lord, the Eternal One says:

Eternal One

Watch carefully! I will judge between one sheep and another, between rams and goats. ¹⁸Are you not satisfied grazing in *blooming* pastures, *by feasting off rich mountain lands*? Do you have to trample all of the pastures with your feet? Are you not satisfied drinking out of clear, *pure, mountain* streams? Do you have to muddy all of the *mountain* streams with your feet? ¹⁹Why should the rest of My flock have to graze in trampled pastures and drink from muddied streams because of your *careless* feet?

²⁰Therefore, this is what the Lord, the Eternal One, says:

Eternal One

Watch carefully! I will personally judge between the fat sheep and the skinny sheep. ²¹Because you bully the weak and push them around with your haunches, shoulders, and horns until they are scattered all over *the mountains,* ²²I will step in and save them. *I will be their rescuer!* They will no longer be hunted and hassled. I will judge between one sheep and another. ²³I will designate one shepherd over the entire flock: My *faithful* servant,

David. He will *watch over them and* take care of them. He will be their shepherd. [24]I, the Eternal One, will be their True God; and My *faithful* servant, David, will be their prince. I, the Eternal One, have spoken.

One of the primary functions of the shepherd is herding. A shepherd shows his concern for the well-being of his flock by keeping them all together, regardless of each animal's whims, and moving them from pasture to pasture safely. The "shepherds" in sixth-century B.C. Jerusalem did not care about the people they led. As a result, most of God's covenant people were scattered among the pagan nations. When God spoke, those attuned to His voice heard His displeasure. They spoke His message, words of rebuke and words of hope. The Eternal One promised to become personally involved: He would bring the miserable shepherds to a miserable end, gather His chosen ones from the nations, and raise up new shepherds to lead His people. Of all the shepherds God promised, there was one Good Shepherd who would overshadow them all. The time was near, the prophets sensed, when the Liberating King, the righteous Branch of David would appear.

Jeremiah 23:1-8

Eternal One | 1 Woe to the shepherds who slaughter and scatter My sheep!

[2]This is what the Eternal One, the True God of Israel, has to say about the shepherds tending My people:

Eternal One

You have scattered My flock, driven them far away, and failed *miserably* at being their caregivers. *In short, you've been careless, wicked leaders*; therefore, I will punish you for *your negligence*, your careless evil. ³I will personally gather the remnant of My sheep from the lands where I have driven them. I will bring them back to their home-pasture where they will be fruitful and multiply. ⁴I will appoint *new, responsible* shepherds to take care of them, and My sheep will no longer be afraid of anything. *These new, responsible shepherds will watch over every single one of My sheep and will not allow any of them* to go missing.

5 Behold! The time is near
     when I will raise up an *authentic*, righteous Branch
        of David,
     an heir of his royal line,
   A King who will rule justly and act wisely
   And bring righteousness to the land.
6 During His reign, Judah will be redeemed
     and Israel will be a safe place again.
   His name will tell the story:
     the Eternal One, our righteousness!

7 So *be ready and* watch carefully. The time is approaching, coming ever so close when no one will say any longer, "As the Eternal One lives, who freed the Israelites out of slavery in Egypt." ⁸Instead, they will say, "As the Eternal One lives, who *ended our exile* and gathered the descendants of Israel out of the north and out of all other countries where He had scattered them." Then the Israelites will live in their own land.

Come of the greatest miracles Jesus performs take place around food and drink. At the wedding in Cana, wine runs like water at His command. On two other occasions Jesus feeds thousands of men, women, and children by multiplying bread and fish. These miracles are told and retold and celebrated in art, music, and literature. But as spectacular as these miracles are, they are only signs pointing to a greater reality. The wine at Cana points to the new wine of the Kingdom. The bread signifies that Jesus is the bread of life. And for those who have ears to hear, both of these miracles anticipate the Lord's Supper and Holy Communion. To provide His disciples with the bread and wine that will always satisfy requires a greater sacrifice.

John 6:26-40

Jesus | 26 | I tell you the truth—you are tracking Me down because I fed you, not because you saw signs from God. ²⁷Don't spend your life chasing food that spoils and rots. Instead, seek the food that lasts into all the ages and comes from the Son of Man, the One on whom God the Father has placed His seal.

Crowd | 28 | What do we have to do to accomplish the Father's works?

Jesus | 29 | If you want to do God's work, then believe in the One He sent.

Crowd	30	Can You show us a miraculous sign? *Something spectacular?* If we see something like that, it will help us to believe. [31]Our fathers ate manna when they wandered in the desert. The *Hebrew* Scriptures say, "He gave them bread from heaven to eat."*
Jesus	32	I tell you the truth, Moses did not give you bread from heaven; it is My Father who offers you true bread from heaven. [33]The bread of God comes down out of heaven and breathes life into the cosmos.
Crowd	34	Master, we want a boundless supply of this bread.
Jesus	35	I am the bread that gives life. If you come to My table and eat, you will never go hungry. Believe in Me, and you will never go thirsty. [36]Here I am standing in front of you, and still you don't believe. [37]All that My Father gives to Me comes to Me. I will receive everyone; I will not send away anyone who comes to Me. [38]And *here's the* reason: I have come down from heaven not to pursue My own agenda but to do what He desires. I am here on behalf of the Father who sent Me. [39]He sent me to care for all He has given Me, so that nothing *and no one* will perish. *In the end,* on the last day He wants everything to be resurrected *into new life.* [40]So if you want to know the will of the Father, know this: everyone who sees the Son and believes in Him will live eternally, and on the last day I am the One who will resurrect him.

* 6:31 Exodus 16:4

*E*ternal life is God's gift to all who put faith in the Good Shepherd. But some refuse to believe despite the beautiful feet that have traveled over mountains and long distances to bring them the good news. You see, faith itself is not our own; it is a gift from God. Oh, it *is* our response to God's gift, but we don't reach inside of ourselves and pull it up from some deep, soul center. We express faith when we hear the glorious message that comes to us courtesy of beautiful feet. We exercise faith when we invoke His glorious name over broken, shattered lives. We articulate faith when in His name we offer a cup of clean, cool water to the poorest of the poor. Where would that faith come from without the beautiful feet that bring the good news?

Romans 10:14-17

[14]How can people invoke His name when they do not believe? How can they believe in Him when they have not heard? How can they hear if there is no voice proclaiming Him? [15]How can they give voice to the truth if they are not sent *by God*? As *Isaiah* said,

> Ah, how beautiful the feet of those who declare the good news of victory, of peace and liberation.[*]

[16]But some will hear the good news and refuse to submit to the truth they hear. Isaiah *the prophet* said,

[*] 10:15 Isaiah 52:7

Lord, who could ever believe it?

Who could possibly accept what we've been told?*

[17]So faith originates in hearing, as we listen to the voice that proclaims the Liberating King.

True shepherds are concerned about one thing—the well-being of their sheep. Jesus, our Good Shepherd, is no different. Unlike other philosophers and teachers of every age, He is not concerned to advance His own ideas or increase His own popularity. He becomes flesh and enters our pasture-world so that His followers will experience *shalom,* peace, well-being. If we believe in Him, then we will be safe from death. If we obey His words and imitate His example, then we will live well in the green pastures the Lord God provides.

John 7:16-18

Jesus | 16 I do not claim ownership of My words; they are *a gift* from the One who sent Me. [17]If anyone is willing to act according to His purposes *and is open to hearing truth*, he will know the source of My teaching. Does it come from God or from Me? [18]If a man speaks his own words, *constantly quoting himself*, he is after adulation. But I chase only after glory for the One who sent Me. My intention is *authentic and* true. You'll find no wrong *motives* in Me.

* 10:16 Isaiah 53:1

While shepherds care for all sheep in the flock, they pay particular attention to the little ones. Throughout His ministry, Jesus spends time with those overlooked by society. He seeks out those in need and liberates them from the burdens oppressing them. Zaccheus is one of these marginal people.

Luke 19:1-10

¹Jesus enters Jericho and seems only to be passing through. ²Living in Jericho is a man named Zaccheus. He's the head tax collector and is very rich. ³He is also very short. He wants to see Jesus as He passes through the center of town, but he can't get a glimpse because the crowd blocks his view. ⁴So he runs ahead of the crowd and climbs up into a sycamore tree so he can see Jesus when He passes beneath him.

⁵Jesus comes along and looks up into the tree [, and there He sees Zaccheus].*

| Jesus | Zaccheus, hurry down from that tree because I need to stay at your house *tonight*. |

⁶Zaccheus scrambles down and joyfully brings Jesus back to his house. ⁷Now the crowd sees this, and they're upset.

| Crowd | (*grumbling*) Jesus has become the houseguest of this fellow who is a notorious sinner. |

* 19:5 The earliest manuscripts omit this portion.

Zaccheus	8	Lord, I am giving half of my goods to the poor, and whomever I have cheated I will pay back four times what I took.
Jesus	9	Today, liberation has come to this house, since even Zaccheus is living as a son of Abraham. [10]For the Son of Man came to seek and to liberate the lost.

Although Jerusalem is the holy city and the temple contains the holy of holies, for many years unholy shepherds lead the nation. They exploit the people and foul God's good name. Only a few days before Jesus is nailed to a Roman cross, He enters the temple, challenges their authority, and condemns their abominable deeds in full view. The power brokers in the high priesthood know what they must do: Jesus has to die. But even as the rich and influential plot His end, children hail Him as the Son of David—a moniker of the coming, Liberating King.

Matthew 21:12-16

[12]Jesus came to the temple. He drove out all those who were buying and selling. He upended the moneychangers' tables and the dove-sellers' benches.

Jesus	13	It is written, "My house will be a house of prayer *for all people*," but you have turned this house of prayer into a den of robbers.*

---

* 21:13 Isaiah 56:7; Jeremiah 7:11

[14]Then the blind and the lame came to the temple, and Jesus healed them. [15]Rings of children circled round and sang, "Hosanna to the Son of David." But the priests and scribes didn't understand. When they saw the *upturned tables, the walking paralytics, and the singing children,* they were *shocked,* indignant, *and angry, and they did not understand.*

Priests and Scribes	16	Do you hear what these children are saying?
Jesus		Yes. Haven't you read your own psalter? "From the mouths *and souls* of infants and toddlers, *the most inno-cent,* You have decreed praises for Yourself."*

*T*here is one final role for the Good Shepherd. He must save His sheep from death and the cold, dark grave. For those who belong to Him and know His voice, death is not the last word. The Good Shepherd lays down His life for the sheep so that death and decay will not touch them.

Psalm 49:7-9, 14-15
[7]One person can't grant salvation to another
    or make a payment to the True God for another.
[8]Redeeming a life is costly;
    no premium is enough, *ever enough,*
[9]That one's body might live on forever
    and never fear the grave's decay.

* 21:16 Psalm 8:2

¹⁴The fate of fools is the grave, and just like sheep,
  death will shepherd them, *feast on them.*
The righteous will rule over them at dawn,
  their bodies, their outward forms, rotting in the grave
  far away from their great mansions.
¹⁵But God will reach into the grave and save my life from its power.
  He will fetch me *and take me into His eternal house.* Selah.

---

*I*f any message is clear in Scripture, if any refrain is memorable, it is this: we are like sheep. At our best and at our worst, we are like sheep. So we need a shepherd. Unfortunately, the human story is replete with thieves, robbers, bad guys, would-be shepherds, con artists, and charlatans. We are vulnerable, easily fooled and exploited by those who come in the back way. But Jesus offers us something much better. He promises to be our shepherd, open and honest, with no agenda but love and no policy but mercy. He is the Good Shepherd because He lays down His life to redeem the entire world. No other will make that promise. Indeed, no other can.

John 10:1-18

| Jesus | 1 | I tell you the truth: the man who crawls though the fence of the sheep pen, rather than walking through the gate, is a thief or a vandal. ²The shepherd walks openly through the entrance. ³The guard who is posted to protect the sheep opens the gate for the shepherd, and the sheep hear his voice. He calls his own sheep by name and leads them out. ⁴When all the sheep have been |

gathered, he walks on ahead of them, and they follow him because they know his voice. ⁵The sheep would not be willing to follow a stranger; they run because they do not know the voice of strangers. *But they know and follow the shepherd's voice.*

⁶Jesus explained a profound truth through this metaphor, but they did not understand His teaching. ⁷So He explained further.

Jesus I tell you the truth: I am the gate of the sheep. ⁸All who approached the sheep before Me came as thieves and robbers, and the sheep did not listen to their voices. ⁹I am the gate; whoever enters through Me will be liberated, will go in and go out, and will find pastures. ¹⁰The thief approaches *with malicious intent*, looking to steal, slaughter, and destroy; I came to give life with joy and abundance.

¹¹I am the good shepherd. The good shepherd lays down His life for the sheep *in His care*. ¹²The hired hand is not like the shepherd caring for His own sheep. When a wolf attacks, snatching and scattering the sheep, he runs for his life, leaving them *defenseless*. ¹³The hired hand runs because he works only for wages and does not care for the sheep. ¹⁴I am the good shepherd; I know My sheep, and My sheep know Me. ¹⁵As the Father knows Me, I know the Father; I will give My life for the sheep. ¹⁶There are many more sheep than you can see here, and I will bring them as well. They will hear My voice, and the flock will be united. One flock. One shepherd. ¹⁷The Father loves Me because I *am willing to* lay down My life—but I will take it up again. ¹⁸My life cannot be taken away by anybody else; I am giving it of My

own free will. My authority allows Me to give My life and to take it again. All this has been commanded by My Father.

*I*f our faith is full of paradoxes, then surely one of those many paradoxes is that Jesus, who is one with God, also serves God. Jesus, the carpenter from Nazareth, gives up the comfort and security of His normal life in order to carry out and serve His Father's will. Jesus, the Liberating King, lives the nomadic life of a shepherd with no place on earth to truly call home. He lives for others. He teaches for others. He heals for others. And most amazingly of all, that Good Shepherd will become the sacrificial lamb for others. He will pour out His life on the altar of the world, be condemned as a seditious criminal and take upon Himself the suffering that is due every last man, woman, and child. He will step consciously and boldly into the position of the suffering servant— a role prophesied hundreds of years before by the prophet Isaiah and a score written at the time of creation—to be slaughtered for the sins of humanity. Although Jesus is the God-man, He chooses to serve and suffer on behalf of the world.

Section Five

The Radiant Glory of the Lord (Radiant)

The melody of the Liberating King continues. The radiant glory of the Lord is being revealed through the story of redemption. We now come to the most chilling moment . . .

Imagine the altar of the entire world—a blood-drenched man nailed against a blood-stained cross. This is the blood of the God-man, Jesus. Sweat drips from His forehead and splatters upon your hand as you kneel before Him. Blood saturates the ground. Your head turns left to hear the moans of His loved ones, but then it is jarred right by cold-hearted orders and taunts of soldiers accustomed to the gore. Meanwhile the defiling cries of the strangers to this God-man send chills up your spine.

You overhear an intimate conversation. Jesus looks to the thief dying next to Him and says, "I promise you that this very day you will be with Me in paradise."[7]

Who is this man? Who in his right mind offers hope to a thief who is doomed to certain death—not years from now, but on this day? Where is this hope coming from?

The thief manages to look at Jesus. Despite the agony of the cross, there is something peaceful, something powerful about His face. In that moment, for the first time in a long time, the condemned man finds peace. He has looked into the face of hope and is found. He has often wondered: *Is*

---

[7] Luke 23:43

there life beyond this miserable mistake of a life that I've lived? Now, he knows.

Perhaps hope is the greatest theme of God's redemption song. But hope is replete with complexities: people and things are not always what they seem to be, and the future rarely turns out the way we expect. This is true of Jesus, who is more than what He seems to be and most certainly is not the image of the Liberating King many expected. However, the vision the prophets project for the coming King is not always crystal clear:

> His leadership will bring such prosperity *as you've never*
> > *seen before—*
> > *sustainable in its integrity,* peace for all time.
> > *This child will keep alive* God's promise to David—
> A throne forever, *right here among us.*
> > He will restore sound leadership
> > that will not, that cannot be perverted or shaken.
> He will ensure justice without fail and absolute equity.
> > Always.
> > *And if you are wondering: how will it happen?*
> The Eternal One, Commander of thousands, is driving
> > *all the stars, furies, fates, and destinies* toward its
> > > realization.
> His passion is unstoppable.[8]

This King will found a nation unlike any on earth, so it is easy to understand why many people await the most powerful political leader the world has ever seen. They are expecting a great and powerful, David-like king. But they forget that David was more than a

[8] Isaiah 9:7

warrior. He was also a singer of songs—songs of redemption and hope.

Ironically, Jesus both fulfills the prophets' vision for salvation and fails to be what His contemporaries expect. How could this be? The Jews hear biblical prophecies with their ears attuned to the sounds of political power. When they hear words like "government" and "king," they anticipate a politically powerful crusader, a royal figure destined to bring justice by crushing the opposition with the same kind of power that conquered Jerusalem in 586 B.C. They are not expecting the power this King wields, a power sourced in heaven and demonstrated through sacrificial service. Our Liberating King will establish justice throughout the world, just as the prophets said, but on heaven's terms, not ours. Even the psalmist recognized how Jesus would bring justice through His words when he wrote:

I will teach in parables;
I will speak of ancient mysteries.
Things that we have heard about,
things that we have known,
which our ancestors declared to us *again and again*.[9]

Matthew further reveals the fulfillment of this prophecy: "Jesus gave all these teachings to the crowd in parables. Indeed, He spoke only in parables in fulfillment of the prophetic words of the Psalms."[10]

Even though He is not the type of king that His contemporaries expected, Jesus is the culmination of the prophecy and the starring

[9] Psalm 78:2-3
[10] Matthew 13:34-35

Vocalist of God's composition. God's Son is the Liberating King who overcomes all of humanity's temptations, guides us to proper belief in God, and defeats death. Through His sacrifice we are set free from the consequences of sin and saved from the still of eternal death.

*J*esus does not come to found a new religion. He comes instead to establish truth. You see, the One God desires that there be one people of God composed of Jews and Gentiles, men and women, haves and have-nots. This has been an important theme in God's composition from the beginning: one God, one people. But Jesus' statements and actions cause division among the people, and most of the leaders don't like what they are hearing.

Jesus and His followers are breaking the most sensible rules and regulations which, they think, are based on God's law. We may fault the Pharisees, scribes, and Sadducees for many things; but of all the Jews in Jesus' day they have the audacity to believe that God has spoken, and they have the courage to believe it matters. So they "build a hedge about the law," adding reasonable rules and traditions—they believe—to make sure they never violate God's law. This is why Jesus is often at odds with the Pharisees—not because they are hopelessly lost, but because they are very near to the priorities and power of the Kingdom. But in hedging God's law with some of their own, they often miss the greater commandments: love God, and love one's neighbor. Two of the reasons the Voice takes on flesh and enters our world are this: to affirm that God has spoken and to show the world what it looks like when God's law is lived perfectly. That is what Jesus means when He says He does not come to abolish but to fulfill the law.

The reality is, however, that with Jesus in the picture, the religious leaders feel their power slipping away. So, instead of giving Jesus a fair hearing, the leaders plot to kill Him. He comes teaching, healing, and saving; but the leaders of the people want to be rid of Him. They cannot—will not—accept that He is their only hope, the long-awaited Liberating King.

Matthew 12:1-14

¹The Sabbath came, and Jesus walked through a field. His disciples, who were hungry, began to pick some of the grain and eat it. ²When the Pharisees saw this, they reacted.

Pharisees		Look! Your disciples are breaking the law of the Sabbath!
Jesus	3	Haven't you read what David did? When he and his friends were hungry, ⁴they went into God's house and they ate the holy bread, even though neither David nor his friends, but only priests, were allowed that bread. ⁵*Indeed,* have you not read that on the Sabbath priests themselves do work in the temple, breaking the Sabbath law yet remaining blameless? ⁶Listen, *One* who is greater than the temple is here.

> ⁷Do you not understand *what the prophet Hosea recorded*, "I desire mercy, not sacrifice."* If you understood *that snippet of Scripture*, you would not condemn these innocent men *for ostensibly breaking the law of the Sabbath*. ⁸For the Son of Man *has not only the*

---

* 12:7 Hosea 6:6

authority to heal and cast out demons, He also has authority over the Sabbath.

⁹Jesus left the field and went to the synagogue, ¹⁰and there He met a man with a shriveled hand. The Pharisees wanted to set up Jesus.

Pharisees | Well, is it lawful to heal on the Sabbath, too?

Jesus | **11** | Look, imagine that one of you has a sheep that falls into a ditch on the Sabbath—*what would you do?*

Jesus | | *(to the Pharisees)* You would dive in and rescue your sheep. ¹²Now what is more valuable, a person or a sheep? *So what do you think—should I heal this man on the Sabbath?* Isn't it lawful to do good deeds on the Sabbath?

Jesus | **13** | *(to the man with the shriveled hand)* Stretch out your hand.

As the man did so, his hand was completely healed, as good as new. ¹⁴The Pharisees went and mapped out plots to destroy Jesus.

*W*ith an occupying Roman army and a cruel Roman governor, most people treasure the hope that the Liberating King will free God's people from foreign rule. Many of the prophecies regarding the Liberator are obscure, but well-meaning people interpret them to suggest that when the Liberating King arrives, the politics will change and Jerusalem will become the center of the world—not an occupied city. In reality that is only part of the truth and Jesus signals this when He enters Jerusalem riding on a donkey as a humble servant, not commanding a chariot as a mighty warrior.

Zechariah 9:9-10

⁹Cry out with joy, O daughter of Zion!
  Shout *jubilantly*, O daughter of Jerusalem!
  Look—your King is coming;
He is righteous and able to save.
  He comes seated humbly on a donkey,
  on a colt, a foal of a donkey.
¹⁰I will dismantle Ephraim's chariots,
  retire the warhorses from Jerusalem;
  send home the archers *to their families in peace.*
He will make peace with the nations;
  His sovereignty will extend from coast to coast,
  from the Euphrates to the limits of the earth.

*J*ust as Zechariah predicted, Jesus rides down the steep incline from the Mount of Olives into Jerusalem on a donkey, a beast of burden. The people, who are for the moment His loyal followers, welcome Him with shouts of joy. With Scripture echoing in their hearts, they hail Him as the long-awaited Messiah, the Liberating King. The children sing psalms to Him, shouting, "Hosanna in the

Matthew 21:1–10

[1]Jesus, the disciples, and the great crowds were heading toward Jerusalem when they came to Bethphage on the Mount of Olives. Jesus stopped and beckoned to two of the disciples.

Jesus | 2 Go to the village over there. There you'll find a donkey tied *to a post* and a foal beside it. Untie them and bring them to Me. [3]If anyone *tries to stop you,* then tell him, "The Master needs these," and he will send *the donkey and foal* immediately.

[4]*He sent the disciples on ahead, so His entry into Jerusalem could* fulfill what the prophet *Zechariah* had *long since* foretold:

[5]Tell this to Zion's daughter,
"Look—your King is approaching,
seated humbly on a donkey,
a young foal, a beast of burden."[*]

[6]So the disciples went off and followed Jesus' instructions. [7]They brought the donkey and foal *to Jesus,* they spread their cloaks on the animals, and Jesus sat down *on them.* [8]The great crowd followed suit, laying their cloaks on the road. Others cut leafy branches from the trees

* 21:5 Zechariah 9:9

and scattered those *before Jesus*. [9]And the crowds went before Jesus, *walked alongside Him*, and processed behind—all singing.

| Crowd | Hosanna, praises to the Son of David! Blessed is He who comes in the name of the Eternal One! Hosanna in the highest!* |

[10]*And that is how* Jesus entered Jerusalem: *on a lowly donkey, with crowds surrounding Him singing praises.* The people of Jerusalem, *to say the least*, noticed this strange parade. They wondered who this could be, *this humble bearded man on a donkey who incited such songs.*

Soon the opposition is able to carry out their plans against Jesus. They accuse Him before the powers-that-be, both Jewish and Roman, in Jerusalem. Ironically, their trumped-up charges are true, just not as they intend. They accuse Jesus of plotting to destroy the temple and replace it. But He has no such plans. He loves the temple. Remember how His parents found Him in its precincts when He was 12 discussing spiritual matters with the temple leaders? Jesus loves God's house, but He knows it will fall under the weight of corrupt leadership and unholy alliances with the Romans. He does not plan to tear it down stone by stone, but He does intend to topple the trappings of a religious system that has lost its way to make room for the believing Gentiles to join the Jews in God's plan for one people.

* 21:9 Psalm 118:26

Mark 14:53-65

⁵³They led Jesus off to *see* the high priest, *who had gathered a council of religious and civic leaders*, legal experts, chief priests, and elders *to hear the evidence and render some decision regarding Jesus*. ⁵⁴Peter followed, at a safe distance, all the way into the courtyard of the high priest; and he sat down with the guards to warm himself at their fire. *He hoped no one would notice.*

⁵⁵The chief priests and other religious leaders called for witnesses against Jesus so they could execute Him, but things didn't turn out the way they had planned. ⁵⁶There were plenty of people willing to get up and accuse Jesus falsely, *distorting what Jesus had said or done*, but their testimonies disagreed with each other, *and the leaders were left with nothing*. ⁵⁷Some gave the following distorted testimony.

Witnesses	58	We heard Him say, "I will destroy this temple that has been made by human hands; and in three days, I will build another that is not made by human hands."

⁵⁹But even here the witnesses could not agree on exactly what He had said.

⁶⁰The high priest stood up and turned to Jesus.

High Priest	Do You have anything to say *in Your own defense*? What do You think of what all these people have said about You?

⁶¹But Jesus *held His peace and* didn't say a word.

High Priest	Are You the Liberating King, the Son of the Blessed One?

| Jesus | 62 | I am. *One day* you will see the Son of Man "sitting at His right hand, *in the place of honor and* power,"* and "coming in the clouds of heaven."* |

63Then the high priest, *hearing Jesus quote the Scriptures supporting His authority*, tore his clothes.

| High Priest | | *(to the council)* What else do we need to hear? 64You have heard the blasphemy from His own lips. What do you have to say about that? |

The verdict was unanimous—Jesus was guilty of a capital crime.

65*So the people began to humiliate Him.* Some even spat upon Him. Then He was blindfolded, and they slapped and punched Him.

| People | | *Come on, Prophet*, prophesy for us! *Tell us who just hit You.* |

Then the guards took Him, beating Him as they did so.

The leaders get their "guilty" verdict and take Jesus to the Roman governor, Pilate, to see if he will agree to a capital sentence. It requires a little convincing; but the foul-natured prefect, Rome's on-the-ground representative, condemns Jesus to death as a political traitor. His sentence—crucifixion. Ironically, it isn't the false witnesses who guarantee a guilty verdict before the high court

---

* 14:62 Psalm 110:1
* 14:62 Daniel 7:13

in Jerusalem. They are too bumbling and ill-prepared for such an important task as breaking the Ninth Commandment. It is Jesus' own testimony that condemns Him. His own words seal His fate.

Isaiah foresaw this incredible moment. The Suffering Servant—young, tender, and unassuming—will weather blows to His body, be afflicted by His enemies, and have His body pierced. Ultimately, He will lay down His precious life, an act of infinite love and sacrifice that redeems us.

Isaiah 53:1-12

¹Indeed, who could ever believe it?

Who could possibly accept what we've been told?

They'd have to see for themselves

when the awesome power and plan of the Eternal One unfolds.

²*Out of what seemed like nothing,*

sterile and empty conditions,

He came. Like a tender shoot

from rock-hard ground.

He didn't look like anything or anyone of consequence—

He had no physical beauty to attract attention.

³So He was dismissed *at best*

and sometimes abused. *We didn't think much of Him,*

this man of constant suffering, grief's *patient* friend.

He kept a low profile.

We simply didn't notice Him most of the time.

⁴Yet *(so small a word for such terrible truth)*

it was our suffering He carried, our pain

and distress, our sick-to-the-soul-ness.

We just figured that God had rejected Him,
    that God was the reason He hurt so badly.
⁵But He hurt because of us;
    because of us, He suffered so.
    Our wrongdoing wounded and crushed Him.
He endured the breaking that made us whole.
    His injuries became our healing.
⁶We had wandered off,
    like shepherdless sheep
    scattered by our aimless striving
    and endless pursuits.
But He was the one who bore the brunt.
    The Eternal One laid on Him*, this silent sufferer,*
    everything that we deserved.

⁷And in the face of it all,
    silence. Not a word of protest, not a finger raised to stop it.
    Like a sheep to a shearing,
    like a lamb to be slaughtered,
    He went—oh so quietly, oh so willingly.
⁸With a perversion of justice He was taken away,
    away from any prison we might recognize.
And who could complain to His people,
    who from His generation was there to cry, "Foul"?
He was, after all, cut off
    from the land of the living,
    smacked and struck *not on His account,*
But because of how My people,
    (My people!) disregarded the lines
    between right and wrong.
They snuffed out His life.

⁹And when He was dead,

 He was buried with disgrace

 in borrowed space (among the rich)

 even though He did no wrong

 by word or deed.

¹⁰*So isn't it odd, hard to understand why*

 the Eternal One felt no compunction about,

 made no apology for crushing Him, wounding Him,

 this innocent Servant of God?

Yet that's it precisely:

 by putting Himself in sin's place,

 in the pit of wrongdoing,

This Servant of God is exalted,

 expanded beyond the limits of an age.

 Because of His Servant,

 the Eternal One's deepest desire

 will come to pass and flourish.

¹¹As a result of the trials and troubles that wracked His whole person,

 God's Servant will see *light* and be content. Because He knows,

 really understands, *what it's about*—

As God says,

 "My just Servant will justify countless others

 by taking on their punishment

 and bearing it away.

¹²*Although I 'desired' it,*

 'felt no compunction,' as you say,

 this sacrifice is not lost on me.

Because He exposed His very self,

 laid bare His soul to the vicious

 grasping of death,

 and was counted among the worst,

 I count Him among the best.

This one, My Servant, has a share in all that is
of any consequence, of any value,
because He stood in the breach,
because He took on the wrongdoing of others
and bore it away."

We have no way of knowing what went through Jesus' mind as He hung on the cross. Thoughts are too private a thing. What we know from the Gospels is that, at some point, His mind and heart turn to the psalms as He endures the pain and suffering of the cross. For centuries the psalms had been sung, chanted, cried, prayed, and shouted to express all the emotions we feel in anguish and in celebration. Jesus is no stranger to suffering or the psalms. In fact, tradition attributes many of the psalms to His ancestor, King David. Not only does Israel's greatest king write psalms, but he also inspires them. A millennium earlier, David records his feelings of abandonment, fear, anger, and hope during one of his military exploits. In David's psalm, we can better understand the feelings of our Liberating King as He sacrifices everything to save His people.

Psalm 69:1-36

¹Reach for me, True God, deliver me.
The waters have risen to my neck;
I am going down!
²My feet are swallowed in this murky bog;
I am sinking—there is no sturdy ground.
I am in the deep;
the floods are crashing in!

³I am weary of howling;
>   my throat is scratched dry.
I still look for my God,
>   even though my eyes fail.

⁴They despised me without any cause;
>   my enemies outnumber the hairs on my head.
They torment me with their power;
>   they have absolutely no reason to hate me.
Now I am set to pay for crimes
>   I have never committed!
⁵O True God, my foolish ways are plain before You;
>   my mistakes—no, nothing can be hidden from You.

⁶Don't let Your hopeful followers be let down because of me, O Lord,
>   Eternal One of heavenly armies;
>   don't let Your seekers be shamed on account of me, O True God of
>   Israel.
⁷I have been mocked when I stood up for You;
>   shame covered my face *like spit in the eye*.
⁸You know my brothers and sisters?
>   They now reject me—as if I never existed.
>   I'm like a stranger to my family.
⁹I am consumed in You, completely devoted to protecting Your house;
>   when they insult You, they insult me.
¹⁰When I fast and mourn for my soul,
>   they deride me.
¹¹And when I put on sackcloth,
>   they mock me.
¹²The *elders* sit at the gate and gossip about me;
>   I am like the *slurred* songs of drunkards.

¹³But Eternal One, I just pray the time is right
    that You would hear me,
And True God, because You are enduring love,
    that You would answer.
In Your faithfulness, please, save me.
¹⁴Pluck me from this shifty muck;
    don't let it take me in!
Pull me from this rising water;
    take me away from my enemies *to dry*.
¹⁵Don't let the flood take me under
    or let Your servant be swallowed into the deep
    or let the mouth of the pit seal me in!

¹⁶O Eternal One, *hear me*. Answer me. Your enduring love is a divine comfort;
    in Your kind mercy, turn toward me.
¹⁷Yes, shine Your face upon me, Your servant;
    put an end to my anguish—don't wait another minute.
¹⁸Come near, rescue me!
    Defend me from my enemies.

¹⁹You know all my opponents;
    You see them, see the way they treat me—
    humiliating me with insults, trying to disgrace me.
²⁰All this ridicule has broken my heart, killed my spirit.
    I searched for sympathy, and I came up empty.
    I looked for supporters, but there was no one.
²¹Even more, they gave me poison for my food
    and offered me *only sour* vinegar to drink.

²²Let them be ambushed at the *dinner* table,
    caught in a trap when they least expect it.

²³Cloud their vision so they cannot see;

> make their bodies shake, *their knees knock in terror*.

²⁴Pour out Your fiery judgment upon them!

> *Make a clean sweep*; annihilate them with Your fury.

²⁵May their camps be bleak

> with not one left in any tent.

²⁶Because they have persecuted the one You have struck,

> add insult to those whom You have wounded.

²⁷Compound their sins;

> *don't let them off the hook!*
>
> Keep them from entering into Your justice.

²⁸Blot out their names from Your book of life,

> so they will not be recorded alongside those who are upright before
> > You.

²⁹I am living in pain; I'm suffering,

> so save me, True God, and keep me safe in high places!

³⁰Your name, True God, will be my song,

> an uplifting tune of praise and thanksgiving!

³¹My praise will please the Eternal One more than *if I were to sacrifice* an ox

> or any *prize-winning* bull. (Horns, hooves, and all!)

³²Those who humbly serve will see and rejoice!

> Those who search for the True God will revive their souls!

³³The Eternal One listens to the prayers of the poor

> and hears the cries of His people held in bondage.

³⁴*All God's creation*: join me in His praise!

> All heaven, all earth, all seas, all creatures of the ocean deep!

³⁵Because the True God will save Zion and rebuild the cities of Judah,

> so that His servants may own and live in them *once again*.

³⁶Their children and children's children shall have *a great* inheritance,

> and those who love His name will dwell in it.

The most universal and haunting of all emotions is loneliness. Jesus hangs alone on that cross, separated from His Father and from those He is dying to save. But His misery and desolation are amplified as onlookers mock Him and taunt Him.

Psalm 42:1-3

¹My soul *is dry and* thirsts for You, True God,
　　as a deer thirsts for water.
²I long for the True God who lives.
When can I stand before Him
　　and feel His comfort?
³*Right now I'm overwhelmed by my sorrow and pain;*
　　I can't stop feasting on my tears.
People crowd around me and say,
　　"Where is your True God *whom you claim will save?"*

The Gospels describe for us the many ways Jesus fulfills the Scriptures. Clearly Jesus' death on the cross for our sins and His resurrection three days later provide a fitting climax to God's covenant story. Everything that happens to Him and by Him serves to resolve the dissonance and disharmony that characterize our essentially human story. But at the moment, His enemies are too busy shouting and mocking to hear the simple harmonies. As they shame Him with taunts and cast lots for His meager possessions, little do they know that He refuses to save Himself so He can save them.

Luke 23:34-37

Jesus | 34 [Father, forgive them, for they don't know what they're doing.]*

Meanwhile, they were throwing dice to see who would win Jesus' clothing. 35The crowd of people stood, watching.

Authorities | *(mocking Jesus)* So He was supposed to rescue others, was He? He was supposed to be the big Liberator from God, God's special Messenger? Let's see Him start by liberating Himself!

36The soldiers joined in the mockery. First, they *pretended to offer Him a soothing drink*—but it was sour wine.

Soldiers | 37 Hey, if You're the King of the Jews, why don't You free Yourself!

f we listen carefully to the Gospels, Psalm 22, more than any other psalm, provides direction and comfort for Jesus as He becomes sin for us on the cross. As God's redemption reaches its pivotal moment, Jesus cries: "My God, My God, why have You turned Your back on Me?"[11] He is not the first man to feel abandoned by God, nor will He be the last. But He is certainly the only perfect man who will ever feel what most people eventually feel: that God has turned His back on us. But if we read the psalm care-

* 23:34 The earliest manuscripts omit verse 34.
[11] Matthew 27:46; Mark 15:34

fully, we realize that more is at stake here than the present feeling of abandonment. God's redemption is just around the corner. For Jesus that is three days.

Psalm 22:1-2, 6-18

[1]My God, My God, why have You turned Your back on Me?
  Your ears are deaf to My groans.
[2]O My God, I cry all day and You are silent;
  My tears in the night bring no relief.

[6]But I am a worm and not a human being,
  a disgrace and an object of scorn.
[7]Everyone who sees Me laughs at Me;
  they say I'm a loser;
  they sneer and mock Me saying,
[8]"He relies on the Eternal One; let Him rescue Him.
  Let Him keep Him safe because He is happy with Him."

[9]But You are the One who granted Me life;
  You endowed Me with trust as I nursed at My mother's breast.
[10]I was dedicated to You at birth;
  You've been My God from My mother's womb.
[11]Stay close to Me—trouble is at My door;
  no one else can help Me.

[12]I'm surrounded by many tormenters;
  like strong bulls of Bashan,* they circle around Me *with their taunts*.

---

* 22:12 a region east of the Sea of Galilee

¹³They open their mouths wide at Me
   like ravenous, roaring lions.

¹⁴My life is poured out like water,
   and all My bones have slipped out of joint.
 My heart melts like wax inside Me.
¹⁵My strength is gone, dried up like shards of pottery;
   My tongue sticks to the roof of My mouth;
   You dump Me in the dust of death.

¹⁶A throng of evil ones has surrounded Me
   like a pack of wild dogs;
   they pierced My hands and ripped a hole in My feet.
¹⁷I count all My bones;
   they gawk and stare at Me.
¹⁸They *made a game out of* dividing My clothes among themselves;
   they cast lots for My clothing.

---

*J*esus prays the psalm—the cry of dereliction—but there is no answer. The heavens are silent. At least for the moment. Jesus, who fed thousands with bread from heaven, who taught His disciples about the coming kingdom of heaven, who is the Son of God come down from heaven, hangs alone on the cross, arms outstretched, embracing the world.

Matthew 27:45-51

⁴⁵And then, starting at noon, the entire land became dark. It was dark for three hours. ⁴⁶In the middle of the dark afternoon, Jesus cried out in a loud voice.

Jesus		*Eli, Eli, lama sabachthani* — My God, My God, why have You forsaken Me?*

Bystanders	47	He's calling on Elijah.

⁴⁸One bystander grabbed a sponge, steeped it in vinegar, stuck it on a reed, and gave Jesus the vinegar to drink.

Others	49	We'll see — we'll see if Elijah is going to come and rescue Him.

⁵⁰And then Jesus cried out once more, loudly, and then He breathed His last breath. ⁵¹At that instant, the temple curtain was torn in half, from top to bottom. The earth shook; rocks split in two.

*T*hat was it. Jesus was dead, and God put an exclamation point on the sentence with an earthquake. Some thought the quake damaged the temple, but there was another possibility—a strange, wonderful possibility. When Jesus died, the veil of the temple was torn, top to bottom, not by the power of the earth shaking, but by the power of the heaven opening a way for us to have permanent access to the Holy One. Measures of silence follow this thunderous ending.

But Jesus' death is only the end of the movement; it is by no means the end of the composition. Three days later God vindicates Him. Jesus rises from death's finality, and out of what seemed to some a failure—His death and the shame of the cross—the church rises.

* 27:46 Psalm 22:1

Matthew 28:1-8

[1]After the Sabbath, as the light of the next day, the first day of the week, crept over Palestine, Mary Magdalene and the other Mary came to the tomb *to keep vigil*. [2]Earlier, there had been an earthquake. A messenger of the Lord had come down from heaven and had gone to the grave. He rolled away the stone and sat down on top of it. [3]He *veritably* glowed. He was vibrating with light. *His clothes were light, white like transfiguration,* like fresh snow. [4]The soldiers guarding the tomb were terrified. They froze like stone.

[5]The messenger spoke to the women, *to Mary Magdalene and the other Mary.*

Messenger of the Lord	Don't be afraid. I know you are here keeping watch for Jesus who was crucified. [6]But Jesus is not here. He was raised, just as He said He would be. Come over to the grave, and see for yourself. [7]And then, go straight to His disciples, and tell them He's been raised from the dead and has gone on to Galilee. You'll find Him there. Listen carefully to what I am telling you.

[8]The women were both terrified and thrilled, and they quickly left the tomb and went to find the disciples and give them this *outstandingly good* news.

Section Six

The Grand Oratorio (Remarkable Things)

We've reached yet another high point in God's grand oratorio. The prophets call it "the last days" because the decisive victory has been won and the powers of sin and death upon the world are drawing to an end. The world itself is not coming to an end; it is destined to be restored to God's original creation, to a place where we commune with Him. This melody of redemption and peace has played softly throughout the piece: often soft and understated, now toward the end, the theme returns in grand and triumphant tones.

In the early movements, God's good creation is corrupted and enslaved to sin. It longs to be free. Then, God's voice echoes through mighty prophets who declare that a Liberator will soon arrive in the world.

When the time is right, the Liberator comes to inaugurate God's eternal salvation. He shepherds and cares for His creation. With signs and wonders, He restores health, reverses death, tames nature, and deals with evil. As His earthly sojourn comes to an end, He becomes a living sacrifice when the powers that rule this world reject Him. After His death, the body of Jesus is taken down from the cross for a proper Jewish burial. Joseph of Arimathea and Nicodemus, secret followers of the Liberating King, place His lifeless body in a rock-hewn tomb that has never held a corpse. On the first day of the week, Jesus' mother (Mary), Mary Magdalene, and other women arrive to discover the tomb open and empty. Heavenly messengers, dual witnesses to an unbelievable act of grace and redemption, announce that He has risen and send the women to tell the other disciples what they have seen. Jesus appears to them and reveals Himself to the disciples. After many proofs that the crucified King has conquered death, Jesus leaves the disciples with the Great Commission and a promise: He will always be with them.

We have not yet heard the end. There is more to come when the Liberator returns as the conquering King. Until then, we can still be part of the Kingdom He is establishing. The character of Jesus, the Liberating King, can be formed in us as we worship, study, and follow the practices—the new wineskins—He has provided. The fruits of the Holy Spirit can pervade every action, thought, and conversation of His followers while we live in a predominately secular culture. Although we now reside as aliens in a world dominated by secular powers, the kingdom of God offers a counterculture that subverts the "bogus world" system with God as our ruler and with practices that reflect His character. We can live lives worthy of Kingdom citizens, but to dwell in the Kingdom, we must be willing to abandon the comforts and securities of mundane life, to dismiss the promises of breathless idols, and to live as if our souls are on fire. We must believe the full message of Jesus.

This melody of the Liberating King invites us all—regardless of our backgrounds, traditions, occupations, or conditions—to be united with Jesus and become a part of the kingdom of God on earth. He sweetly and fiercely summons our sleeping souls and weaves them into His divine vision of His kingdom. He empowers individuals to awaken the souls within, and He instructs all Kingdom citizens to embark upon a divine and eternal mission in, for, and of the eternal Kingdom.

The melody of redemption and the truth of the Kingdom bring the truest freedom. We are called to live in this freedom, to break free of elitist, exclusive cages—boundaries built by laws and rules—and live in truth, love, and worship of God. Jesus' offer of a new life will continue to fuel and inspire the human spirit for as long as we choose to truly live as humble and confident members of Jesus' eternal kingdom.

As we listen to the song, we hear of the Liberating King who has become the world's greatest—and most mysterious—teacher. He has spawned centuries of unresolved controversy, generated millennia of unanswered questions, and attracted the skeptical, incredulous eyes of the world.

*E*ven before His death and resurrection, Jesus knew who He was, where He came from, and where He would go; He did not conceal His royal claims even though He knew they would infuriate Jewish and Roman leaders. These leaders were judging His every word and movement, searching for a way to convict Him of a capital crime. Instead of hiding His true identity, the Liberating King warned them of a time when the tables would be turned and He and His Father would judge them.

John 8:13-19

Pharisees	13	Jesus, what You are claiming about Yourself cannot possibly be true. The only person bearing witness is You.
Jesus	14	Even if I am making *bold* claims about Myself—*who I am, what I have come to do*—I am speaking the truth. You see, I know where I came from and where I will go *when I am done here.* You know neither where I come from nor where I will go. ¹⁵You spend your time judging *by the wrong criteria*, by human standards, but I am not here to judge anyone. ¹⁶If I were to judge, then My

judgment would be based on truth, but I would not judge anyone alone. I act in harmony with the One who sent Me. [17]Your law states that if the testimonies of two witnesses agree, their testimony is true. [18]Well, I testify about Myself, and so does the Father who sent Me here.

Pharisees | 19 | Where is the Father *who testifies on Your behalf*?

Jesus | | You don't know the Father or Me. If you knew Me, then you would also know the Father.

*E*verything about the Christian faith stands or falls with Jesus' resurrection. The prophets foretold of a day when death will give way to life, when those who sleep in the earth will awake to everlasting life.[12] Jesus' resurrection is the first installment of that blessed hope. On that first Easter, the flesh and blood of our Liberating King becomes eternal. If that isn't true, our faith is useless. Our hope is based completely on the transformed body of our Lord.

Jesus' resurrection is the critical moment of His reign as our Liberating King. All creation hangs in the balance as death gives way to life. As the divine plan unfolds and moves toward its final movement, He will overthrow worldly powers and conquer all of His enemies, including death. When He conquers death, all who belong to Him will share in His victory so that death loses its ultimate power. Then, when all things are right and at peace, He will give His kingdom over to God.

[12] Daniel 12:2-3

1 Corinthians 15:12-28

[12]Now, if we have told you about the Liberating King (how He has risen from the dead *and appeared to us fully alive*), then how can you *stand there and* tell us there is no such thing as resurrection from death? [13]*Friends,* if *you say* there is no resurrection of the dead, then *you are saying that* even the Liberator hasn't been raised, [14]and if that is so, then all our preaching has been for nothing and your faith *in the message* is worthless. [15]And what's worse, all of us *who have been preaching the gospel* are now guilty of lying against God because we have been spreading the news that He raised the Liberating King from the dead (which must be a lie if what you are saying about the dead not being raised is the truth). [16]*Please listen.* If *you say,* "the dead are not raised," then *what you are telling me is that* the Liberating King has not been raised. *Friends,* [17]if the Liberator has not been raised *from the dead,* then your faith is worth less *than yesterday's garbage,* you are all doomed in your sins, [18]and all *our dearly* departed who trusted in His liberation are left decaying *in the ground.* [19]If we have based this lifetime on our hope in the Liberator *(and He is truly dead),* then we, *of all the fools around,* deserve the world's pity.

[20]But the truth is that the Liberating King was raised from death's slumber and is the firstfruits of those who have fallen asleep *in death.* [21]For since death entered *this world* by a man, it took another man to make the resurrection of the dead *our new* reality. [22]*Look at it this way:* through Adam all of us die, but it's also true that through the Liberating King all of us can live again. [23]But this is the order *of how it will happen*: the firstfruits (the Liberator's *awakening*) is followed by all those who belong to Him at His coming, and [24]then the end will come. After He *has conquered His enemies and* shut down every rule and authority vying for power, He will hand over the Kingdom to God, the Father *of all that is.* [25]And He must reign as King until He has put all His enemies under His

feet. [26]The last to be destroyed is death itself [27]because *Scripture says*, "You placed everything on earth beneath His feet."*

(Although it says "everything," it is clear that this does not also pertain to God, *who created everything* and made it all subject to Him.) [28]Then, when all creation has taken its rightful place beneath God's sovereign reign, the Son will follow, subject to the Father who exalted Him over all created things; then, God will be God over all.

*B*ut how can we be resurrected and live forever? Our bodies are flesh and blood, subject to illness and decay; but when "the last trumpet" calls, we will be transformed, metamorphosed— caterpillar to butterfly, mortal to immortal. We will overcome death, sin's sad effect, because the Liberating King saves us from its bondage.

1 Corinthians 15:50-58

[50]Now listen to this: brothers *and sisters,* this present body is not able to inherit the kingdom of God any more than decay can inherit that which lasts forever. [51]Stay close, because I am going to tell you something you may have trouble understanding: we will not all fall asleep with death, but we will all be transformed. [52]*It will all happen so fast,* in a blink, a mere flutter of the eye. The last trumpet will call, and the dead will be raised from their graves with a body that does not, cannot decay. All of us will be changed! [53]We'll step out of our mortal clothes and slide into immortal bodies, *replacing everything that is subject to death with eternal life.* [54]And, when we are all redressed with bodies that do not, cannot

* 15:27 Psalm 8:6

decay, when we put immorality over our mortal frames, then it will be as *Scripture* says: *"Life everlasting* has victoriously swallowed death."*

⁵⁵"Hey Death! What happened to your big win? What happened to your sting?"* ⁵⁶Sin *came into this world*, and death's sting *followed.* Then sin *took aim at* the law and gained power *over those who break the law.* ⁵⁷Thank God, then, for Jesus the Liberating King who brought us victory *over the grave.*

⁵⁸My dear friends, stay firmly planted—be unshakable—do many good works in the name of God, and know that all your labor is not for nothing when it is for God.

Not all will fare well in the world that is coming. While the resurrection brings life—everlasting, abundant life—to those who belong to the Liberating King, those who oppose Him will face certain judgment. But this warning is not new. Prophets and poets have spoken and written of it since ancient times. Those who will cast aside the gentle tyranny of God's love will find that they too will be cast aside, eternally separated from God's wide mercy.

Psalm 2

¹*You are wondering:*
>What has provoked the nations to embrace chaos and outrage?
>Why are the people making plans to pursue their own vacant and
>>empty greatness?

²Leaders of nations stand united;
>rulers put their heads together,

---

* 15:54 Isaiah 25:8
* 15:55 Hosea 13:14

plotting against the Eternal One and His Anointed *King*,
trying to figure out
³How they can throw off the gentle tyranny of God's love
and advance their own power and kingdoms.

⁴*At first,* the Power of heaven laughs *at their silliness.*
The Eternal mocks their *ignorant selfishness.*
⁵But *His laughter turns* to rage, and He rebukes them.
As God displays His *righteous* anger,
they begin to know *the meaning of* fear.
He says,
⁶"I am the One who places My King over Zion, My mount of holiness."

⁷I am telling *all of you the truth. I have heard* the Eternal One's
decree. He said clearly to Me:
"You are My Son. Today I have become Your Father."
I was chosen by His Spirit.

⁸*His offer to me defies generosity. He withholds nothing.*
He said:
"The nations shall be Yours for the asking,
and the entire earth will belong to You.
⁹They are Yours to crush with an iron scepter,
Yours to shatter like cheap, clay pots."

¹⁰So leaders, kings, and judges, be wise, and be warned.
¹¹*There is only one God,* the Eternal One;
worship Him with respect and awe;
take delight in Him and tremble.

¹²Bow down before *God's* Son.

If you don't, you will face His anger *and retribution*,

    and you won't stand a chance.

For it doesn't take long to kindle royal wrath,

But blessings await all who trust in Him.

    They will find God as a gentle refuge.

Psalm 110

A song of David.

¹The Eternal One said to my Lord,

    "Sit here at My right hand,

    in the place of honor and power,

And I will gather Your enemies together,

    lead them in on hands and knees;

    You will rest Your feet on their backs."

²The Eternal One will extend the reach of Your rule

    from Your throne on Zion.

    You will be out in enemy lands, ruling.

³Your army will come to You as volunteers that day;

    no conscripts, no mercenaries will be found among them.

    They will be a sight to see:

That day You lead Your army,

    noble in their holiness,

    as if the dawn herself gave birth to them;

The power of youth—like dew in the morning sun.

⁴The Eternal One has sworn an oath;

    His mind cannot be changed:

"You are a priest always—
　　in the *honored* order of Melchizedek."
[5]The Lord is at Your right hand;
　　on the day that His fury comes *to its peak*,
　　You will see kings crushed.
[6]You will see the dead *in heaps at the roadside*,
　　whole countries full of bodies—
　　in valleys and on hillsides.
Rulers and military leaders will lie among them
　　without distinction.
　　This will be His judgment of the nations.

[7]There is a brook along the way.
　　He will stop there and drink,
And when He is finished,
　　He will raise His head.

O̧nly one person is worthy to rain that judgment on the earth—
the Liberating King. He is the Lion of the tribe of Judah, the
Son of David who becomes for us the sacrificial lamb. As He steps
forward to crack the seals and unleash God's final, just judgments
on the world, John the emissary learns the truth about Him. He sees
the mystery that has been working from the beginning. The Good
Shepherd becomes the defenseless lamb who freely gives Himself
for us. His sacrifice makes Him the only worthy judge.

But the final act of saving is yet to be completed, and the victory celebration promises to be grand. A marvelous picture is
painted of that final act when His ultimate sacrifice is crowned as
the greatest accomplishment of all time. Imagine you are present

when the Lamb steps forward, as the only One who is worthy. Then rejoice with the saints throughout the ages as He fulfills His destiny as Liberating King: Ruler of rulers and Master of masters.

Revelation 5:1-14

John | 1 | And then I saw a scroll in the right hand of the One seated upon the throne, a scroll written both on the inside and on the outside. It had been sealed with seven seals. ²Then a mighty heavenly messenger proclaimed with a loud voice,

Mighty Messenger | Who is worthy to break the seals and open the scroll?

John | 3 | No creature *of creation* in all heaven, on all the earth, or even under the earth could open the scroll or look into its *mysteries*. ⁴Then I began *to mourn* and weep *bitterly* because no creature *of creation* was found who was worthy to open the scroll or to look into its *mysteries*. ⁵Then one of the elders consoled me,

One of the 24 Elders | Stop weeping. Look there—the Lion of the tribe of Judah, the Root of David. He has conquered and is able to break its seven seals and open the scroll.

John | 6 | I looked and between the throne and the four living creatures and the *24* elders stood a Lamb who appeared to have been slaughtered. The Lamb had seven horns and seven eyes (the eyes are the seven Spirits of God sent out over all the earth). [7]The Lamb came and took the scroll from the right hand of the One seated upon the throne. [8]And when He took it, the four living creatures and 24 elders fell prostrate before the Lamb. *They worshiped Him, and* each one held a harp and golden bowls filled with incense (the prayers of God's holy people). [9]Then they sang a new song.

Four Living Creatures and 24 Elders

You are worthy to receive the scroll,
>to break its seals,
>because You were slain.
With Your blood You redeemed for God
>people from every tribe and language,
>people from every race and nation.
[10] You have made them a kingdom,
>You have appointed them priests to serve our God,
And they* will rule upon the earth.

John

[11] When I looked *again,* I heard the voices of heavenly messengers (numbering myriads of myriads and thousands of thousands). They surrounded the throne, the living creatures, and the elders.

Thousands of Messengers

[12] *(with a great voice)* Worthy is the Lamb who was slain.
>*Worthy is the Lamb* to receive authority
>and wealth and wisdom and greatness
>and honor and glory and praise.

* 5:10 Some texts read "we."

John	13	Then I heard every creature in heaven and on earth and beneath the earth and in the sea and all things in them *echoing the messengers.*
Every Creature		To the One who sits on the throne and to the Lamb be blessing and honor and glory and power throughout the ages.
John	14	And the four living creatures *kept on repeating*:
Four Living Creatures		Amen. *Amen.*
John		And the elders fell down and worshiped.[*]

The drama of redemption is nearly complete. But the enemies of God do not go peacefully. All that remains is for the humble King who rode into Jerusalem on a donkey to return and finish what He started. But this time He comes on a white stallion. He is dressed for battle, His robes dipped in blood, a constant reminder of the martyrs' sacrifices. He comes with the heavenly armies to claim what is rightfully His as King of kings and Lord of lords.

[*] 5:14 Some texts add "Him who lives forever."

John | 11   *In what seemed to be no time at all*, I looked up and saw that heaven had opened. Suddenly, a white horse appeared. Its rider was called Faithful and True, and with righteousness He exercised judgment and waged war. [12]His eyes burned like a flaming fire, and on His head were many crowns. His name was written *before the creation of the world,* and no one knew it except He Himself. [13]He was dressed in a robe dipped in blood, *stained red by the blood of the martyrs, and* the name He was known by was The Word of God. [14]And the armies of heaven, outfitted in fine linen, white and pure, were following behind Him on white steeds. [15]From His mouth darts a sharp sword with which to strike down the nations. He will rule over them with a scepter made of iron. He will trample the winepress of the fury of the wrath of God, the All Powerful. [16]And there on His robe and on His thigh is written His name: King of kings and Lord of lords.

Once He has overthrown the principalities and powers, once He has judged evil and wickedness decisively and definitively, the Liberating King returns to heaven to a glorious scene. All creatures join in a magnificent chorus of praise: "Hallelujah! Praise the Lord! The Lord, God Almighty reigns!" they chant. The dead are there, raised and immortal. The prisoners are there, free and joyful. The

weak and despised are there, standing strong and proud. They have
been redeemed by the blood of the Lamb. Together they are the
King's bride, made ready for a banquet for the ages.

Revelation 19:1-10

John	1	*The scene changed.* After this, I heard the great sound of a multitude *echoing* in heaven.
Multitude		Praise the Lord! Salvation and glory and power *truly* belong to our God,
	2	for true and just are His judgments. He has judged the great whore who polluted the *entire* earth with her sexual immorality, And He has vindicated the blood of His servants, *the martyrs*.
John	3	Again praise *spilled from heaven*:
Multitude		Praise the Lord! The smoke rises up from her *ruins* forever and ever.
John	4	And the 24 elders and four living creatures fell on their faces and worshiped God who reigns on the throne.

Four Living Creatures and 24 Elders	Amen, Praise the Lord!

Voice from the Throne	5 Give praise to our God,
	    all of you, God's servants,
	    all who reverence Him,
	    small and great.

John	6 And I heard what seemed to be an immense crowd speaking with one voice—it was like the sound of a *roaring* waterfall, like the sound of clashing thunder.

Multitude	*(in unison)* Praise the Lord!
	For the Lord our God,
	    the All Powerful, reigns *supreme*.
	7 Now is the time for joy and happiness.
	    He deserves all the glory we can give Him.
	    For the wedding feast has begun,
	The marriage of the Lamb to His bride has commenced,
	    and His bride has prepared herself *for this glorious day*.

John	8 She had been given the finest linens to wear, linens
	      bright and pure,
	    woven from the righteous deeds of the saints.

Heavenly Messenger	9 Write this down: "Blessed are those who are invited to the marriage banquet of the Lamb." What I am telling you are the true words of God.

John	10	At that, I fell down at his feet to worship him, *but he refused my praise.*
Heavenly Messenger		Stop it. Don't you see? I am a servant like you and your brothers and *your sisters*, all who hold fast to the testimony of Jesus. Address your worship to God, *not to me!* For the testimony about Jesus is *essentially* the prophetic spirit.

And so the music of the ages draws to a close. Throughout God's composition the melody of His wondrous grace plays, fulfilling His plan. Although He does send messengers and emissaries, the decisive acts are His and His alone. He reveals the movements of His composition one piece at a time, sometimes with measures of silence lasting hundreds of years. But slowly, in His perfect timing, God shows His great love for us. He gives us His Son—the Liberating King, the good shepherd, and the spotless lamb—who is destined to rule all kings. God uses Him to show us perfection and then He lays our imperfections on Him so that we might become worthy of His perfect righteousness.

God has provided all that is needed to complete the oratorio of our redemption by the Liberating King, but each of us still has a part to play. Will we follow our Conductor?

Wake up, beloved. The kingdom of God is at hand.
May we always hear His melody.

Index